The Gospel Goes To Broadway

The Gospel Goes
To Broadway

Inspiration in Songs from Broadway Musicals

James R. McCormick

2013

This book is dedicated to the members of Church of the Good Shepherd in Arcadia, California, First United Methodist Church in Philadelphia, Mississippi, Parkway Heights United Methodist Church in Hattiesburg, Mississippi, First United Methodist Church in Tupelo, Mississippi, and Big Canoe Chapel in Big Canoe, Georgia. It was for you that these messages were originally written, and it is because of your enthusiastic response that this book has been published. To you all I express my love and gratitude!

James R. McCormick

CONTENTS

Introduction   ix

My Fair Lady
   Wouldn't It Be Loverly   1
   The Rain In Spain   9
   I Could Have Danced All Night   17
   I've Grown Accustomed To Her Face   25
Oliver
   Where Is Love?   33
   Consider Yourself At Home   41
The Sound of Music
   The Hills Are Alive With the Sound of Music   47
   How Do You Solve a Problem Like Maria?   55
   Climb Every Mountain   63
   My Favorite Things   71
Music Man
   Goodnight My Someone   79
   'Til There Was You   85
South Pacific
   A Cockeyed Optimist   93
   Happy Talk   101
   You've Got To Be Carefully Taught   107
   This Nearly Was Mine   115
Singing In The Rain
   Singing In the Rain   123
The King and I
   Whistle a Happy Tune   129
Fiddler On The Roof
   Tradition!   137
   Sunrise, Sunset   143
   Do You Love Me?   151
   If I Were a Rich Man   157
   Miracle of Miracles   165
Annie
   Tomorrow   173

Man of La Mancha
    The Impossible Dream   181
Carousel
    You'll Never Walk Alone   189

Introduction

This book began to form in May of 1978. I was pastor of Church of the Good Shepherd in Arcadia, California. The local high school was staging a production of "Fiddler on the Roof" and it seemed that everyone in town was caught up in the excitement of it. I decided to take hold of that excitement and preach a series of sermons based on several of the songs in that delightful musical. I had always loved Broadway musicals and the movie adaptations that often followed. It is not surprising then that I hit upon this combination of theater and sermon; nor is it surprising that this combination became some of the most loved and memorable of all the sermons I have preached. What is a bit surprising to me is that, as far as I know, this has not been done by others.

When I preached the sermons based on the songs from "Fiddler", and when I saw the response they generated, I was motivated to explore other songs from other musicals. So, for the rest of my ministry, I have featured a series of sermons from Broadway musicals almost every year, usually in the summer. I would introduce the musical and the setting of the song and then someone would sing the song featured for that day. When the song had been sung, I would make the connection with the gospel story. And always, the Sundays we "went to Broadway" were among the best attended of the year!

There is a good rationale for this approach. Each year there are many plays and musicals produced in theaters around the world. Writers keep writing and producers keep looking for next year's hit. Some are successful and some are not. Most are not. But if you will look at the really successful ones, you will note that they all have at least one thing in common. In addition to being well written, directed, and produced, they all find a way to touch the depths of the human spirit. They deal with "stuff" that is real, and the audience senses that it is real. I have long believed that all truth is God's truth, so wherever you find truth, you find God. If the dramas and musicals on Broadway deal with life's truths in such a way as to touch the heart, there must be something there of God's truth. So, it makes sense to come at the gospel from that perspective.

A quote which has been bouncing around in my mind for some time is this: "All windows look out on the same world." If that is true, as I believe it is, then the Broadway "window" and the New Testament "window" are both attempting to look at, experience, and interpret the same world. Where do those windows come together to make sense of that world? My answer: in this book, of course!

This book seeks to find the place of commonality between Broadway and the gospel. And, once we develop the eyes and ears necessary to see and hear the gospel in Broadway songs, perhaps we can begin to recognize the hand of God in all of the other commonplace experiences of life as well.

I am indebted to the musicians in several congregations who made the stories in these songs come alive and sent us out from worship singing, whistling, and humming. Music has a way of touching us in the deep places of our lives. Thanks to you for making that happen! I am also grateful to the members of the congregations where these sermons were first preached. It was your enthusiastic response and your encouragement that motivated me to put them into print. And, I thank Liz Donovan-Davis for her invaluable help in producing this volume, as well as the previous, "Does It Look and Sound Like Jesus?"

James R. McCormick

Wouldn't It Be Loverly?

Matthew 4:1-4

The story began at the end of the first century B.C. Ovid, a Roman writer, wrote a story about a sculptor who fell in love with a female statue he had made. The story was re-visited by George Bernard Shaw, in his 1913 play, "Pygmalion." It was given new words and music by Lerner and Loewe when their musical, "My Fair Lady" opened on Broadway in 1956. It was then made into a memorable movie starring Audrey Hepburn and Rex Harrison in 1964. Whatever else you might want to say about it, the story is durable!

The musical opens in a square in London, outside a theater, where the opera, "Faust" has just concluded. Eliza Doolittle is a young cockney woman who is barely scraping out a living by selling flowers to the elite of London's upper crust. Eliza's life has been hard. Growing up in a dysfunctional family, with a ne'er do well alcoholic father, who beat her, she had to begin looking out for herself when she was far too young. Because of that, she is tough and street-smart despite her tender years. She never had the luxury of a good education. Clearly she is a commoner, with that tell-tale cockney accent. She butchers the English language!

And that's where Professor Henry Higgins comes in. Professor Higgins is an expert on phonetics, the science of speech. In the opening scene, he demonstrates his ability, by listening to a person's speech, to identify where they were born and where they have lived. We can all do that to some extent when we ask, "You're not from around here, are you?" But Higgins is a master of it. He is a sophisticated, well-to-do, confirmed bachelor and the more we learn about him, the more we question whether or not anyone could bear to live with him! He is arrogant, condescending, and rude. But he plays no favorites. He treats everyone badly. In fact, he has been so insensitive for so long he is genuinely surprised when people are offended by his behavior. But he is good at what he does – researching and teaching the science of phonetics.

There, in the square, is also Colonel Hugh Pickering, himself a linguist, who has come to London to meet Henry Higgins. They have much in common: the finest education, a love of language, and their stature as wealthy men in the higher echelons of English society.

On that evening, Professor Higgins is doing research out in the square. With notebook in hand, he is taking notes of the various dialects he hears, especially the language of Eliza Doolittle. When she learns that he is watching her and taking notes, she fears that he is a policeman and that she is in trouble with the law, although she protests that she has done nothing wrong. She begins to cry, protesting loudly, and a crowd gathers. Her sounds offend his ears, so Higgins says, "Cease this detestable boo hooing instantly, or seek the shelter of another place of worship." She says, defiantly, "I have a right to be here if I like, same as you!" Higgins says, "A woman who utters such depressing and disgusting noises has no right to be anywhere, no right to live."

He doesn't let up. He continues, "She is a prisoner of the gutters, condemned by every syllable she utters. She should be taken out and hung, for the cold blooded murder of the English tongue!"

Out of the crowd, Colonel Pickering comes to Eliza's defense, and Pickering and Higgins meet. Each has heard of the other and has admired the other's work from a distance. Pickering reveals that he has come to London to meet Higgins, and so the Professor invites him home with him for an extended visit. During their conversation, Higgins boasts of his ability to teach. In fact, using Eliza Doolittle as an example, he says that within six months he could transform her into such a lady that she could mix comfortably with London's nobility. In fact, he boasts, he could pass her off as a duchess at the Embassy Ball! Eliza overhears the conversation, and files the information away for later use.

When Higgins and Pickering and the rest of the elite people have left the square, only the working people are left. And, as marginalized people often do, they deal with their situation by making fun of privileged people. One person sings, "It's rather dull in town. I think I'll take me to Paree." Another sings, "The mistress wants to open up the castle in Capri. My doctor recommends a quiet summer by the sea!" As they fantasize about a life they would like but cannot have, they sing, "Wouldn't it be loverly?"

Eliza joins in the singing, but her dreams are a bit more modest. Let's listen:

> "All I want is a room somewhere, far away from the
> cold night air.
> With one enormous chair, Aow, wouldn't it be loverly?
> Lots of chocolates for me to eat, lots of coal makin' lots
> of 'eat.
> Warm head, warm hands, warm feet, Aow, wouldn't it
> be loverly?
> Aow, so loverly sittin' abso-bloomin-lutely still. I would
> never budge 'till spring
> Crept over me windowsill.
> Someone's 'ead restin' on my knee, warm and tender
> as 'e can be,
> Who takes good care of me, Aow, wouldn't it be
> loverly?

I suppose we all fantasize about the life we would like to have, about what it would take to make life "loverly" for us: the bulging stock portfolio, the big house, the new car, the perfect spouse, model children and grandchildren.

Eliza's desires were pretty basic, weren't they? She wanted a room to live in, a comfortable chair to sit in, enough coal to keep her warm, and time to sit in her chair and rest. She was tired. The only luxury in her list was "lots of chocolates for me to eat." Can you imagine? What she wanted was some candy to sweeten the bitterness of her life. Basics.

Are you familiar with the late Abraham Maslow and his Hierarchy of Needs? Maslow was a psychologist who has identified basic human wants and needs. He says that the foundational needs are physiological and safety needs – food to eat, water to drink, air to breathe, protection from the elements. These are all survival needs. Closely related are safety needs…we need to believe that we are safe and protected. Maslow contends, and I agree, that these needs are so basic that we seldom even think about other needs until these needs have been met. Eliza and her friends on the square are concerned about the basics –about survival.

There's a whole world out there like that. There are millions of people who are just hoping to get through one day and live to see the next. That's a different world from the one we live in. There are hordes of people who long for the things we take for granted. Let's let Eliza Doolittle remind us of those people for whom basic survival is a blessing.

But, give Eliza credit. She doesn't stop with that. She wants more than that. So, she begins to dream about a loving relationship. She sings, "Someone's 'ead resting on my knee, warm and tender as he can be, who'll take good care of me. Aow, wouldn't that be loverly!" Eliza understood something I talk about a lot…life is about relationships. And she wants that, a relationship with someone warm and tender, someone who will love her enough to take good care of her. That's something she has never had. Not even from her own father. She knows that life will never be really "loverly" for her if she is all alone. Life requires relationship…loving and being loved.

But, even if Eliza had her warm room, her comfortable chair with time to sit in it, even if she had her chocolates and her "someone" warm and tender, even if she had all of that, it wouldn't be enough. There is more to life than that.

Tell me, what do you dream about? If you were to make a list of the things you would like to have added to your life to make it "loverly," what would they be? We have the basics. We don't have to worry about survival issues, so what do we want added? What would make life good for you?

A lot of people dream of "stuff." If I could just possess this. If I could just acquire that. But stuff will never make us happy. What a cruel joke life plays on us, to give us what we want, only then for us to discover that it is not what we really wanted. Whoever dies with the most toys does not win. Those who *have* to have a lot of toys have died long before they stopped breathing. I remember something I read years ago and have not forgotten, "A person is wealthy in proportion to what they can do without." It's okay to want nice things. It's okay to enjoy nice things. It's not okay to *have* to have things in order to be happy. Do you understand the difference? Things will never satisfy us.

A lot of people dream of being in circumstances other than the ones they are in. But, again, circumstances do not make us happy and fulfilled. We don't always have control of our circumstances, do we? We can become sick, suffer financial reversals, be betrayed or disappointed by others, suffer through a tornado, a lightning strike, or a bridge collapse. Circumstances are not always controllable. The question is, what kind of person are you bringing to whatever circumstances you find? Are you the kind of person able to prosper, no matter what your circumstances? Or are you a perpetual victim of your circumstances? No, even good circumstances are not enough.

Some people dream of changes in their family or their friends. If only my spouse were like this, if only my parents acted like that, if only my children would do what I want them to do. If only - if only - if only the important people in my life were different! I know people who are miserable because they insist upon changes that are beyond their control. Listen: you can't change other people. The only person you can control is you. You can control what you do with those people who will not change to your specifications. You can change your attitude. You can change your behavior. But you can't change *them*. If that's your dream, you will be disappointed.

What do you want? What do you think will make life "loverly" for you? That's an important question, because the size of your life is determined by the size of the thing you think will make you happy. Oh, I forgot to warn you, I just said something important, so let me repeat it: the size of your life is determined by the size of the thing you think will make you happy.

Let's listen to what Jesus said about that. Just after Jesus' baptism, he went out in the wilderness to sort out his life and to listen to God's voice about the direction he was to go. He was met there by the tempter, the one who knows how to attack us wherever we appear to be weak. Jesus had been in the wilderness for forty days and he was hungry, so the tempter said, "If you are the son of God, command these stones to be turned into bread." Listen to what Jesus said in reply because it's important. He said, "It is written, 'one does not live by bread alone, but by every word that comes from the mouth of God.'" Jesus was quoting from Deuteronomy, what the people of Israel were told after their wanderings in the wilderness.

There they were fed by quail that fell from the sky, and by manna that was gathered fresh every morning. But they were reminded that food was not enough. Life is more than that. "One does not live by bread alone."

So, Jesus was reminding himself and us that life is not just about survival and safety needs. Notice that he did not say they are unimportant. They are just not enough. I appreciate so much the realism of Jesus. He knows of our need for food and air and water and shelter and clothing. And, throughout his ministry, he showed a concern for all of that. Jesus ministered to the whole person. If people were hungry, he fed them. If they were sick, he healed them. He was not concerned just for their souls, he was concerned for *them* And, all who follow in his footsteps must also be concerned about all the things that affect God's children for good or ill. That's why we want to feed the hungry, heal the sick, house the homeless, and educate the illiterate. We are to see to it that all people's physical needs are met. That's important. It's just not enough.

Jesus said that we are to live by bread. But not only bread. We are to live by every word that comes from the mouth of God. Now, originally, that referred to the scriptures of Israel, the commandments that had been given to Israel through Moses. It means that. But it means more than that. What it means is that we are to live by all that comes to us from God. The thing that provides a foundation for life and the thing that completes life is the experience of God Himself and all the gifts of love that God provides.

That was the primary theme of Jesus' teaching: the Kingdom of God, the primacy of God, the centrality of God. You can have everything else in life worth having, but if you don't have a right relationship with God you will never be fully happy and satisfied. That's the way it is, because that's the way God created it to be. You and I were made to live in a loving, trusting, obedient relationship with God and then in a loving and mutually helpful relationship with one another. And the quality of life is determined by the quality of those relationships.

Jesus said it so many times in so many different ways. He said, "Seek first the Kingdom of God, put that first and then everything else that you need will be yours as well." Jesus was saying that if you have God at the center of your life, you can live pretty well without almost everything else. But if God is not at the center of your life, you are not going to be fully happy, no matter what else you have. As someone has said, "Until a person finds God and is found by God, he begins at no beginning and works to no end."

Wouldn't it be "loverly" if we understood that? Wouldn't it be "loverly" if we opened our hearts to the reality of that: God, that loving, forgiving, blessing God made known in Jesus at the very center of life! You have that and everything else in life is made more beautiful, more enjoyable, and more life-giving as a result.

Professor Henry Higgins was a teacher. He believed that he could change a person's life by what he put in their head and by what he put on their lips. He believed he could transform a commoner into a duchess by teaching her how to speak.

Well, Jesus was a teacher too. But, Jesus would say, however important education is, what you put into your heart is more important than what you put into your head. No matter what else you know, unless you know who you are and whose you are, you don't know nearly enough. Jesus didn't teach us how to *pronounce* words. He taught what words were *most worth* pronouncing, words like God, grace, forgiveness, faith – words of meaning.

Jesus would never be content just to pass Eliza off as a duchess. No, not just pass her off. He would *make* her into a new person, a unique, loved, blessed child of God. And, until that happens in her life, and in ours, no matter what else happens, it will never be enough.

Listen to Jesus: "One shall not live by bread alone, but by every word that comes from the mouth of God." When we live like that, it's... What better way is there to say it? It's loverly!

Prayer: God, our Father, come to us now and give us what we need. Give us all we need not just to survive, but to live, to live in right relationship with You and with others, as the cherished sons and daughters of God. In Jesus' name we pray. Amen.

The Rain in Spain

Hebrews 1:1-2

In the previous chapter, the story of "My Fair Lady" concluded with Eliza singing "Wouldn't It Be Loverly." I wrote about the things we think would make life "loverly" for us. We concluded that "stuff" won't do it. Good circumstances won't do it. Longing for changes in other people won't do it. Only a right relationship with the God made known in Jesus, and the right relationships made possible with others as a result, will make life "loverly" for us. It took me longer to say it, but that's what the last chapter was about.

Professor Henry Higgins had boasted to Colonel Pickering that he could make Eliza into a lady by teaching her how to speak properly. He could pass her off as a duchess at the Embassy Ball, he bragged. Eliza overheard his boast, and remembered it. No doubt it added fuel to her dreams of who she could yet be and dreams of what she could yet do with her life.

So, in this scene, Eliza had dressed herself up in her finest clothes, even washed her face and hands, and had taken a cab to the home and studio of Professor Henry Higgins. Higgins was explaining his research and teaching methods to Pickering, and they were listening to recordings of various vowel sounds when Eliza was ushered into the room.

As soon as he heard her voice, Higgins said, "No, no, no, this is the girl I saw in town last night. She's of no use to me. Be off with you, I don't want you!" She replies, with no small amount of dignity, "I've come for lessons, and I'll pay for them too, make no mistake." Higgins says, "And what do you expect me to say?" She replies, "Well, if you were a real gentleman, you would ask me to sit down, I would think."

Higgins turns to his friend and says, "Pickering, should we ask this baggage to sit down, or should we throw her out of the window?" "Aow, I won't be called baggage. I'm offering to pay, just like any lady," Eliza says. Pickering approaches her and asks, "What do you want, my girl?" Eliza replies, "I want to be a lady in a flower shop, instead of sitting on the corner on top of Court Road. But they won't take me unless I talk more genteel. And, he said he could teach me. Well, here I am, willing to pay. I'm not asking any favors. I know what lessons cost as well as you do, and I'm willing to pay!"

Pickering says, "Higgins, I'm interested. What about your boast that you could pass her off as a duchess at the Embassy Ball? I'll say you're the greatest teacher alive if you can make that good. I'll bet you all the expenses of the experiment that you can't do it. I'll even pay for the lessons!"

Higgins responds, "She's so deliciously low, so horribly dirty, I'll take it. I'll make a duchess out of this draggle-tailed gutter snipe. We'll start today…this moment!" And so, the task began.

Hour after tedious hour, day after exhausting day, they went at it. Pronouncing, or *trying* to pronounce vowels. A-E-I-O-U. Higgins would say, "Say 'A'." Eliza would respond, "Aeee". He had her reading with pebbles in her mouth, ala Demosthenes. He had her practice the phrase, "How kind of you to let me come!" again and again. He had her sitting in front of a device with a gas flame. When she pronounced a word beginning with "H" properly the flame would enlarge. When she dropped her "H's" it would remain the same. He gave the model: "In Hartford, Hereford and Hampshire, hurricanes hardly happen." Eliza responded: "In Artford, Ereford, and Ampshire, urricanes ardly appen." The flame didn't move!

Higgins said, "Repeat after me, 'The rain in Spain stays mainly in the plain'." And, of course she butchers it. Over and over again they go at it. She becomes tired and they both become irritable. Higgins says, "Every night before you go to bed, where you used to say your prayers,

I want you to say, 'The rain in Spain stays mainly in the plain' 50 times. You'll get much further with the Lord if you'll learn not to offend His ears!"

Day after day the same grating sounds came from Eliza's mouth. It seemed that they were getting nowhere. One night, exhausted and discouraged, she finally said, "I can't. I'm so tired!" And then, just when it seemed that the cause was lost, there was a dramatic breakthrough. Let's listen:

Eliza: "The rain in Spain stays mainly in the plain". Higgins: "By George, she's got it! By George she's got it!"

Wow! After all the work, and after all the failures and disappointments, she finally got it! I can understand them celebrating and dancing when the breakthrough came. "By George, she's got it!"

Now, what had made the difference? What had turned failure into success? What was the reality behind the breakthrough?

Well, repetition for one thing. Hour after hour, day after day, repeating the same vowels, the same sentences. Repetition is a key to learning, isn't it? Whether it's playing scales on the piano, practicing our putting, or pronouncing words correctly, repetition is a large part of our learning. Do you remember how many times you said the multiplication tables before getting them right? Do you remember how many times you dribbled a golf ball along the ground before getting it into the air. Do you remember learning the alphabet, the drilling over and over again? We've done that at our house recently as we have learned the alphabet again, along with our 4 ½ year old granddaughter. A, B, C, D, E, F, G, I 'm sure that repetition was a large part of Eliza's learning. She kept saying, "The rain in Spain stays mainly in the plain" until she got it right.

Example is another part of learning. She kept hearing Professor Higgins' impeccable pronunciation, and that of Colonel Pickering, and even the household staff. They all spoke good English. And day after day, week after week, she was exposed to it. It had to make a difference. I have said it again and again: "We tend to become like that with which we associate on a continual basis." So, it makes sense to decide who we want to be, and then intentionally surround ourselves with the influences which will help us to become that person, while avoiding those influences which will take us in other directions.

So much of the good in my life is because I have been exposed to good examples. Of course, I had to use my freedom to embrace those examples. I will always be grateful for those people who lived lives of excellence in my sight, and gave me an example of what it means to be authentically human, and lovingly Christian. Example is important!

And inspiration: the right motivation, someone believing in us, believing in who we can be, and what we can do...those are important too. I almost missed it in the musical, "My Fair Lady". I was so caught up in the humor and the music that, for the first few times I saw this delightful musical, I missed them. Shame on me. I missed some of the most important elements in the story!

On the night of the breakthrough, Eliza was at the point of giving up, saying that she couldn't go on. She was tired. She couldn't do what Higgins asked of her. Listen to what he said then: "I know your head aches. I know you're tired. But think of what you're trying to accomplish. Just think of what you're dealing with. The majesty and grandeur of the English language is the greatest possession we have. The noblest thoughts that ever flowed into the hearts of men are contained in the extraordinary, imaginative, and musical mixture of its sound. And that's what you've set yourself out to conquer, Eliza. And, conquer it you will!"

After letting the Professor's words sink in, Eliza properly said, "The rain in Spain stays mainly in the plain." That was inspiration. That was motivation. And, perhaps most importantly, it was affirmation. Even after all of his previous put downs, in this moment Higgins says that he believes in her. He believes she can do it. And so she did!

God, we need that! Whatever is good about us, whatever is noble about us, I'll bet we can explain in exactly that way. Someone has believed in us enough to call forth the best from within us. And I'll tell you, there is power in that!

I know there is no other way to account for my life. I remember those countless Sunday school teachers who, week after week, let me know that they believed in me. They believed in who I could become. They cared enough to invest their time, to teach me those memory verses and what they mean. My life today bears their imprint.

I remember a Scout Master, Mr. Frank Williams, who was the leader of Troop 2 in Meridian, Mississippi. Mr. Frank believed that I could become an Eagle Scout, and he wouldn't let me off the hook until I did. I was older than many of the boys and there were some of those merit badges that gave me trouble, but Mr. Frank stayed after me until I reached my goal. He believed in me.

I remember Miss Annie Ellis, and Mrs. Johnston, and Bob Bergmark and other teachers who invested their lives in teaching. Never paid what they were worth, and often going unappreciated, I cannot overstate their influence in my life. I am a different person, a better person today because they believed in me.

And Houston Jenks, my band director, took a skinny little kid, lost in the middle of the trumpet section, singled me out, challenged me, and told me he believed in me enough to make me section leader of the trumpet section. I had to succeed. I had to succeed because Mr. Jenks believed in me.

I think about those members of the first small congregations I served as pastor. I was so young, so inexperienced, and so unskilled. But they let me know that they believed in me. They believed I could learn to preach, and to be an effective pastor. Their trust gave me much needed encouragement. My parents, especially my mother, told me how much she loved me and believed in me again and again. And Patricia, who has believed in me as few others have. Knowing my faults better than anyone, she still has believed in me. Knowing all of that, how could I let any of those people down? Whenever I have been tempted to compromise, to cut corners, and to be less than I know I should be, I have remembered their faith in me. By their love and trust they have called forth the best from within me, and my life is different, my life is better as a result.

Do you remember what Elizabeth Barrett Browning said in one of her letters to Robert? She wrote, "I love you not only for what you are, but for what I am when I am with you." I can say that, too, about all of the people in my life who have believed in me.

So, those factors, at least, were a part of the change we have seen in Eliza Doolittle. And they are factors in virtually all change for the better in all people: Repetition, example, and the kind of encouragement that comes from someone saying, "I believe in you!"

That brings us to the main thing I intended to say in this chapter. While writing it, I followed other thoughts that came to me, I trust from God, but this is the thing that came to me first when I started thinking of this series. Listen now: "My Fair Lady" is a dramatic, theatrical presentation of the story of the Bible. It's a metaphor for the ancient story of the God who, century after century, with amazing patience and persistence, has reached out to His people to tell us who He is and who we are, and to call us into a right relationship with Himself and with others. That's the story of the Bible, and that's the story of "My Fair Lady".

Think about it. Higgins wants to teach Eliza how to speak like a lady. So, with dogged determination he teaches her. She fails to get it. So, he tries again. Again, she fails to get it, so he tries again. He tries this and that. He works in this way and in that way. Weeks and months, he keeps at it, until finally she gets it. And they dance all over the stage in celebration!

Just so, the story of the Bible is the story of a God who seeks us out, to tell us His truth, and to call us to Himself. Periodically we seem to "get it", and there is celebration. I can almost hear God saying, "Thank Me, they've got it!" Then He takes it a step further and tries to impart some greater truth. We get part of it, but not the whole of it. So, He tries again. With remarkable divine patience and persistence, God reaches out to us. And, every time there is a break through, there is celebration in heaven! I'll bet there is dancing even in heaven when we experience a bigger God, a larger truth, a more inclusive and redemptive expression of love.

Look at the Biblical story: first people believed in many gods, but the one God continued to work with them until there was that dramatic breakthrough, "Shema Yisrael", "Hear O Israel, the Lord our God, the Lord is one!" And the first monotheistic people on the face of the earth were called into being. But those people who had gained such insight began to think of themselves as chosen from all the people of the world for special privilege. They were better, more loved than others, they thought. God had to work with them, wrestle with them, really, to help them see that they were called not for special privilege, but for special responsibility. They were to be "a light to the nations". And, people once thought that God said that they were to love their neighbors and hate their enemies. Well, they were half right, but God had to work to correct their limited vision. Many people once thought that God was mostly demanding, not giving, wanting them to jump through a lot of religious hoops or he would severely punish them. It took awhile to convince us that God is not in the punishment business, but in the redemption business. And, a lot of people haven't gotten that straight yet! Throughout Biblical history there have been those little people who wanted to bring God down to their size, to create God in their image, to make God endorse their values, second their motions, to reduce the life of faith to a religion of rules and regulation and propositions, missing the point of it all, until Jesus came and gave us the truth for all who will hear it and embrace it. Someone asked him one day to name the greatest commandment. Listen to his magnificent answer: "You shall love the Lord, your God will all your heart, and mind, and soul and strength. That is the first and great commandment. And a second is like it: You shall love your neighbor as yourself." Listen now: Jesus said, "On those two, rest all the law and the prophets", in other words, that's a summary of the whole of the Bible. Do you hear it? It's about right relationships. And God has sent prophets, and priests, and messengers of all kinds to get through to us, to help us to understand and to respond in faith. He did that patiently and persistently for centuries. And, finally, when everything was prepared, God sent Jesus to us, the fullest expression of Himself and of what He intends for His world. Because Jesus is the fullest expression of God's truth, we find ourselves putting everything to that test, asking again and again, "Does it look and sound like Jesus?"

Isn't that what the scripture from Hebrews says? "Long ago, God spoke to our ancestors in many and various ways by the prophets, but in these last days He has spoken to us by His Son." That's the story of the Bible. And, in the strange way my mind and heart are wired, that's pretty much the story of "My Fair Lady". Patience, persistence, believing, and hoping. And, the result is, we get it!

Listen: the good news of the Christian gospel is not that we believe in God, but that God believes in us. God believes in all we can become by His grace. And, when we get it, when we become who God believes we can be, there is great rejoicing in heaven. "They've got it. Finally, they've got it!" And, when that happens, it's loverly!

Prayer: We thank You, our Father, for not giving up on us. Century after century, patiently, persistently, You have stayed with it, revealing Yourself to us, calling us to a trusting relationship with You and loving relationships with one another. Stay with us, we pray. Keep working with us until finally we "get it", and become who we're supposed to be. Hear us as we pray in the name of Jesus, who has made You known. Amen.

I Could Have Danced All Night

Psalms 30:11-12

In the last chapter there was a breakthrough in the "My Fair Lady" story. Eliza Doolittle was a young cockney girl who supported herself modestly by selling flowers on the street corner. Professor Henry Higgins, a researcher and teacher of phonetics, the science of speech, had met her, noted her common language and said that it was her flawed speech that was holding her back. He boasted to his friend, Colonel Hugh Pickering, that he could transform her into a lady. He said that within six months he could pass her off as a duchess at the Embassy Ball by teaching her to speak properly.

Eliza heard the boast, and it triggered dreams of a better life for her. So, she showed up at his studio for lessons, offering to "pay like any lady." Pickering had bet Higgins all the expenses of the experiment and the voice lessons that he could not make good on the boast. Higgins took the challenge and the work began.

It was a difficult task! Eliza butchered the English language and her street environment reinforced that butchering every day. But, once she gave herself over into the hands of Professor Higgins for teaching, she was surrounded by people who enunciated properly and used grammar impeccably. And they all worked hard at it. Hour after tiring hour, day after exhausting day they went at it: reciting the alphabet, pronouncing vowels, and even practicing reading with marbles in Eliza's mouth. Just before the breakthrough, Eliza was at the breaking point. The professor had said, "Repeat after me: 'The rain in Spain stays mainly in the plain'." Eliza said, "I can't. I'm so tired."

But, after a final appeal from Higgins, in which he talked about the majesty and grandeur of the English language, and about how all the noblest thoughts of mankind flowed through its sounds, he said, "And that's what you've set yourself out to conquer, Eliza. And, conquer it you will!" After letting that sink in, Eliza said it correctly for the first time, "The rain in Spain stays mainly in the plain."

Higgins jumped up from his seat and said, "She's got it! By George, she's got it." Eliza and Higgins and Pickering sang and danced all over the stage in celebration. And, Eliza said all the challenging words, "In Hartford, Hereford and Hampshire, hurricanes hardly happen." And she said it correctly. She said, "How kind of you to let me come." And she got it right. And she said, again, "The rain in Spain stays mainly in the plain." And they all grinned, and they sang the words, and Eliza danced with Higgins, and Eliza danced with Pickering, and Pickering danced with Higgins, and it was all wonderful!

It was so wonderful in fact, and they were now so confident of the progress they had made, they made plans to take Eliza out to mingle with the upper crust of London society. They talked excitedly about going to the races at Ascot where everybody who was anybody would be. Wow! Talk about a breakthrough!

After all of that, it was bedtime. Actually it was well past bedtime, and everyone was exhausted. So, one by one they headed off to bed. That is, everyone but Eliza. With her heart pounding, the excitement lingering, the satisfied smile still on her face, Eliza knew she couldn't sleep even if she tried. So, once again, she begins to sing. Let's listen…

"Bed, bed, I couldn't go to bed, My head's too light to
try to set it down
Sleep, sleep, I couldn't sleep tonight, not for all the
jewels in the crown.
I could have danced all night, I could have danced all
night
And still have begged for more. I could have spread my
wings
And done a thousand things I've never done before.

I'll never know what made it so exciting, why all at
once my heart took flight,
I only know when he began to dance with me
I could have danced, danced, danced all night."

What a delightful song! As a part of the song, Eliza sang, "I'll never know what made it so exciting; why all at once my heart took flight." She didn't know, so let's help her out. Let's try to decide why it was that she was so excited that she couldn't sleep, and could have danced all night.

I suppose, like most people, when I first saw and heard "My Fair Lady", I assumed that Eliza was singing about romance, that she had fallen in love with Henry Higgins and that she could have danced all night because she was dancing with him. There is that fanciful streak in most of us that would like to find a romantic relationship in every play and movie. And that may have been present, to some extent, even a large extent. But, the more I have seen the musical and the more I have thought about it, the more I have come to believe that the romantic part is not all there is.

I believe Eliza was so excited because she had worked at an important task, and, against huge odds, she had been successful at it. She had done something really worth doing, when others had said it couldn't be done. She was proud of herself, and for good reason. That accomplishment gave promise of so much more to come: a new life for her, new opportunities, both financial and social. That night had been really something!

And, in addition, she had won the approval of her teacher. Henry Higgins himself had said, "She's got it! By George, she's got it!" After months of hard work, and tons of disappointment and disapproval, she had finally succeeded, and even her taskmaster had said so. I tell you, that's worth celebrating. Something like that makes you want to dance!

In the scripture cited at the beginning of this chapter, the Psalmist wrote: "You have turned my mourning into dancing; you have taken off my sackcloth and clothed me with joy." Well, doesn't that describe what happened to Eliza? There she was, failing, discouraged, ready to give up, when suddenly there was that breakthrough. Her failure was turned into success and her mourning changed into dancing! She was so happy that she danced all over the stage. Everyone gave Henry Higgins the credit, and he did help. But listen, I'm about to say something important:

whenever mourning is changed into dancing, whenever that happens, it really is God at work. In fact, whenever anything good happens to us, it is God. Unfortunately a great many people don't know that, and so they don't know who to thank. But God is the source of all good. Don't ever forget that.

That brings us to the first question I want to ask: what is it in life that excites you? What is it that thrills you? What is it that makes you so happy you want to dance? It had better be something. If you have lost the capacity for that kind of happiness, or if, for you, life is just routine, hum drum, boring, you might just as well jump in the hole and let them cover you up, because you are dead.

There are lots of things that excite me, some more important than others. But I enjoy life. I intend to go to heaven, but I am in no hurry to get there, because I enjoy living life right here and now. For one thing, I am a sports fan. I get excited about my team coming from behind and pulling out a victory at the end. I work so hard to help them over the hump that I often find myself being tired as a result. But it's a good tired.

I enjoy playing golf and launching a long drive down the middle of the fairway. I enjoy hitting an approach shot stiff to the pin and then sinking the birdie putt. That's exciting! I enjoy winning a tennis match against an opponent I'm not supposed to beat. I enjoy beating a younger opponent who calls me "sir" on the court. When I go out to play either tennis or golf, Patricia often says, "Have fun!" I say in response, "You know how you spell fun. It's w-i-n!" (I have been told that I can be a bit competitive!) I really enjoy sports!

I love this wonderful world God has created and entrusted to us, a world of trees, flowers, lakes, and butterflies. I love the songs of birds, the wonders of a starry sky, and the glories of sunsets!

And, I can get excited about music. I don't do it much any more, but when I was playing my trumpet regularly, I could sit in an orchestra and play Glenn Miller or Duke Ellington arrangements for hours. I'd rather do that than eat. And, singing one of those marvelous anthems with a good choir, that's a religious experience for me. I can be moved to tears by beautiful, meaning filled music.

But, as much as I enjoy those things, there is a much higher level of enjoyment and excitement when it comes to my family. I enjoy being with my family! There is not much in this world that thrills me more than receiving a kiss and a hug from Patricia, from our children or grandchildren, and having them say, "I love you. I'm proud of you." It doesn't get much better than that!

And, to share worship with a faithful congregation, that's exciting to me. I love it when we are together to praise God, to thank God, to offer prayers to God, and then for me to have the privilege of telling the story, that old, old, story of Jesus and his love. I am sure that it is no mystery that I enjoy preaching and teaching. I get excited about that. I love to preach and teach. I hate to prepare because preparing is hard work. But, I'm smart enough to know that I won't enjoy the preaching and teaching very much if I don't prepare in advance, so I do it because I love the privilege of telling the story. And, I especially love it when, after classes, someone says to me, "For the first time in my life I can read the Bible and begin to understand it." Or, "For the first time in my life, I know what the Christian gospel is about!" Or, for someone to say, "God is real in my life, and I am closer to Him than I've ever been. Thank you!" There is no greater thrill and no greater satisfaction in life than that.

What is it that excites you? What makes you so happy that you want to dance? Those are important questions. Their answers will tell you a great deal about yourself. I said in the first chapter in this series that "the size of your life is determined by the size of the thing you think will make you happy." I believe that, and this is another way of saying it: the size of your life is determined by the size of the thing that excites you, the thing that brings you joy. So, what does that for you? Eliza was so excited that she could dance all night. At least part of the reason was that she had accomplished something important and something that could make life so much better for her. What does that for you?

Here is a second question: to what audience do you play as you live your life? Whose approval do you seek above all others? Eliza danced because she had won the approval of Henry Higgins, and his approval was important to her. Whose approval do you seek?

Do you seek the approval of your parents, your spouse, your friends, your boss, or your colleagues at work? And, do the ones you are trying to please call forth the best from within you? Or, do they ask for compromise, lowering your standards, being less than you know you should be? It's so tempting isn't it, to go through life twisting ourselves into whatever shape we think the significant others in our life want from us. And that can be either good or bad depending upon the ones whose approval we are seeking.

I was talking with someone recently who told me, "My boss told me that I would never advance very far in the company if I held too rigidly to my standards." This person asked the boss, "But you're a Christian. Have you made compromises in your values to get where you are?" The boss replied, "Yes, I have. I'm not proud of it, but I have." How sad! He wasn't proud of it, but he also didn't have any intention of changing it. This employee was being asked to be less of a person in order to win the approval of company executives. How sad, and how destructive it can be, when someone important to you seems to want you to be less than you can be.

I read recently about a man whose job took him on the road a lot. He said that every time he checked into a hotel room, he placed a picture of his wife and children on the bedside table. Whenever he had a question about a course of action, he said he would put it to that jury. What would they think about it? Their approval was important to him, and it helped him make right choices.

Whose approval is most important to you? Whoever it is, their opinion and their values are shaping your life in significant ways. One thing that has always been important to me is to be able to go home at night, look in the mirror, and feel good about what I see. I know me pretty well. I know who I want to be as a child of God. So, it's important to feel good about the person who looks back at me from the mirror.

There was a poem about that in one of Ann Landers' columns. I clipped it out and saved it. Listen:

> "When you get what you want in your struggle for self
> And the world makes you king for a day,
> Just go to a mirror and look at yourself
> And see what *that* man has to say.
>
> For it isn't your father or mother or wife
> Whose judgment upon you must pass,
> The fellow whose verdict counts most in your life
> Is the one staring back from the glass.
>
> Some people might think you're a straight-shootin'
> chum
> And call you a wonderful guy.

But the man in the glass says you're only a bum
If you can't look him straight in the eye.

He's the fellow to please, never mind all the rest,
For he's with you clear to the end,
And you've passed your most dangerous test
If the guy in the glass is your friend.

You may fool the whole world down the pathway of years
And get pats on the back as you pass,
But your final reward will be heartache and tears
If you've cheated the man in the glass."

Do you like yourself? Do you approve of yourself? Do you approve of the direction you are going in life? Important questions.

Most importantly, do you seek the approval of God? Set aside all the rest for a moment and ask, are you becoming who God created you to be? Are you growing and becoming in such a way that your life looks and sounds more like Jesus every day?

If God is not the audience you are playing to, if God is not the primary one whose approval you seek, then you are cheating yourself and everyone who loves you. You're selling out too cheaply.

God is the One, and the only One who can make life good for us. That's what the Psalmist was saying in our scripture for the morning. "You have turned my mourning into dancing; you have taken off my sackcloth and clothed me with joy." Just think about that. Turning sadness into joy. Turning grief into gladness. Turning emptiness into fullness. Turning fear into faith. Turning death into life. Only God can do that for us. And He can do it for us only when we look to him for grace, and guidance, and strength. And only when, above all else, we seek God's approval.

When I teach preaching to young preachers, I ask them about their audience. Whose approval are they seeking? I always tell them that, in my experience, congregations will settle for far less than they are capable of doing. They can cut corners on their preparation and do a shoddy job of preaching and there will still be those who will pat them on the back and tell them they are great. The most important thing I tell them is this: "The best of all the preachers plays to an audience of one:

God. We seek God's approval. And, if God approves of what we do, then we will be the best we can be."

I can think of nothing I would rather hear, either in this life or in the next, than to hear from God, "Well done, well done, good and faithful servant." I tell you, you seek that, and your life will be shaped in the best of all ways. Then, when you hear that "Well done, good and faithful servant", when you hear that, you will feel like dancing, all night, all the next day, and throughout all eternity!

I leave the questions with you, and important questions they are: what is it in life that excites you and makes you want to dance? And, whose approval, finally, do you seek?

Prayer: Loving Father, we do want to pursue the right goals. We do want to get excited about the right things. And, when we are at our best, above all else, we do want Your approval. So, right here and now, touch us by Your Spirit. Call us again to Yourself. And give us all we need to be who we were created to be, Your cherished, blessed children. In Jesus' name we pray. Amen.

I've Grown Accustomed To Her Face

Philippians 4:8-9

Professor Henry Higgins had boasted, "I can take this flower girl off the street and within six months pass her off as a duchess at the Embassy Ball!" His new found friend, Col. Hugh Pickering had bet him that he could not do it. Higgins had accepted the bet, and the game was on. After working diligently for months, Eliza had made enough progress that they decided to try her out at the Ascot races. She did fairly well, with only a few gaffes, and Higgins passing off her misstatements as the latest "small talk." And, there, at the races, Eliza captivated Freddy Eynsford-Hill, who fell head over heels in love with her. After that, he spent hours each day outside the Higgins house. He wrote love notes to her, sent her flowers, and even sang the lovely, "On the Street Where You Live."

After the races they went back to work, straightening out the rough spots, to get her ready for her grand debut: the Embassy Ball. The long awaited day came. She went to the ball and became the center of attention. She was elegant, and beautiful, and charming. She danced with the Prince of Transylvannia. Everyone was talking about her, wondering who she was. And, her performance was so good, that even Professor Higgins' protégé, also a teacher of phonetics, was deceived. After listening carefully to her speech, he declared that she could not be English because her speech was too polished. She had had excellent instruction, but obviously, she was really Hungarian, and royalty at that!

It was a triumphant evening! The entourage returned to the Higgins house laughing and celebrating the victory. Higgins had made good on his boast and Pickering broke into song, singing, "You did it! You said that you would do it and indeed you did!" The household servants joined in the celebration and singing. Everyone was rejoicing, that is, everyone but Eliza. She stood at the side of the room, unnoticed and ignored, as if invisible. They talked about her as if she were not even present.

Then, at the end of the celebrating song, Higgins puts his feet up on his desk and says, "Well, thank God that's over. I can go to bed without dreading tomorrow!" After a few minutes they all went off to bed, leaving Eliza alone, and she began to cry. Higgins comes back in, saying to himself, "What have I done with my slippers?" Eliza looks up and, in anger, throws his slippers at him, saying, "Take your slippers, and may you never have a day's luck with them."

Incredulously, Higgins says, "What on earth...Have I done you wrong?" "No," she says, "Nothing wrong with you. I've won your bet for you, haven't I? That's enough for you. I don't matter, I suppose." "*You* won my bet!" he replies. "You presumptuous insect, *I* won it!" "What's to become of me?" she asks. Higgins replies, "How the devil should I know what's to become of you?" "You don't care," she says. "I don't mean as much to you as them slippers." "Those slippers," he corrected. "Where am I to go? What am I to do? What's to become of me?" she asks.

"O, so that's what's bothering you," he said. "Well, I wouldn't worry about that if I were you. You can settle yourself somewhere or other, I am sure. You might marry, you know." After thinking about that, he said, "I dare say my mother might find some fellow or other who would do very well." Having said that, he goes off to bed, again leaving Eliza quite alone.

With Higgins gone, she begins to think of how she had been devalued. Her anger boils over and she begins to sing, "Just you wait, Henry Higgins, just you wait. You'll be sorry, but your tears will be too late. You will be the one it's done to, but you'll have no one to run to, just you wait, Henry Higgins, just you wait!"

In the wee hours of the morning, Eliza packs her things and leaves. She goes back to the square where she once sold flowers, but no one recognizes her. She is a lady now, and doesn't belong in her former world. She wonders if she belongs anywhere.

The next morning, the members of Professor Higgins household get out of bed only to discover that Eliza had gone. They had not expected that. They went into a panic, calling the police about their missing person. Higgins says, "What in all of heaven could have prompted her to go, after such a triumph at the ball? What could have depressed her? What could have possessed her? I cannot understand the wretch at all!" Finally, in distress, Higgins goes to his mother's house to seek comfort.

He did not know that Eliza was there, having tea. And his mother, graciously, had said to Eliza, "Remember, you not only danced with a Prince last night. You behaved like a Princess." When her son came in and found Eliza and his mother together, he treated Eliza contemptuously and condescendingly, as usual. His mother said, sweetly to Eliza, as she poured the tea, "However did you learn good manners with my son around?" Eliza said, "It was very difficult. I should never have known how ladies and gentlemen behaved if it weren't for Colonel Pickering. He always showed me that he felt and thought about me as if I were something better than a common flower girl." Briefly glancing at Higgins, sulking in the corner, she continued, "The difference between a lady and a common flower girl is not how she behaves, but how she is treated. I shall always be a flower girl to Professor Higgins because he always treats me as a flower girl and he always will. But I know I shall always be a lady to Colonel Pickering because he always treats me as a lady and he always will."

Higgins defends himself, saying that he does not intend to change who he is or what he does. He explains, "Colonel Pickering treats a flower girl like a Duchess, and I treat a Duchess like a flower girl. The question is not how I treat you, but do I treat anyone else any better?" Eliza says, "I don't care how you treat me, but I won't be passed over. I can get along without you. Don't you think I can't!" She then thinks out loud about marrying Freddy, who loves her. She talks of supporting Freddy by teaching phonetics, according to the methods she learned from her Professor. After exchanging other words which get them nowhere, she says, "Goodbye, Professor Higgins. You shall not be seeing me again!" And she leaves.

When it sinks in that she has gone, Higgins cries out, "Mother!" When his mother appears, he says, plaintively, "She's gone!" "Well, of course, dear," she says, "what did you expect?" "What shall I do?" he asks. "Do without her, I suppose," she replies. "Well, I shall!" he exclaims. And he storms out.

Walking at a brisk pace, venting his anger, all the way home he goes over things in his mind, his feelings fluctuating. And he begins to sing. Let's listen…

> "I've grown accustomed to her face, she almost makes
> the day begin.
> I've grown accustomed to the tune that she whistles
> night and noon,
> Her smiles, her frowns, her ups, her downs
> Are second nature to me now, like breathing out and
> breathing in,
> I was serenely independent and content before we
> met,
> Surely I could always be that way again, and yet,
> I've grown accustomed to her look, accustomed to her
> voice,
> Accustomed to her face."

> Speaking: "Marry Freddy! What an infantile idea. What
> a heartless, wicked, brainless thing to do. But she'll
> regret, she'll regret it. It's doomed before they even
> take the vow!
> But, I'm a most forgiving man;
> The sort who never could, ever would
> Take a position and staunchly never budge.
> A most forgiving man.
> But, I shall never take her back.
> If she were crawling on her knees.
> Let her promise to atone; let her shiver, let her moan;
> I'll slam the door and let the hell-cat freeze!
> Marry Freddy… Ha!
> But, (singing) I've grown accustomed to her face."

After singing his song, Higgins goes into his studio and looks around. It seems empty somehow. He sits down and begins to console himself by listening to recordings of Eliza's voice.

At the end of George Bernard Shaw's play, "Pygmalion," Eliza leaves Professor Higgins and marries Freddy. Shaw was adamant about it, never allowing Eliza to go back to one who had treated her so badly, insisting that she deserved to be loved!

But, in Lerner and Loewe's version, Eliza returns to the Higgins house, and finds him sitting there alone, listening to her recorded voice. Before he knows she is standing there, she turns off the recording and says, "I washed me face and hands before I come, I did." Higgins says, "Eliza?" Then, with a satisfied grin, he settles down in his chair and says "Where the devil are my slippers?" And with that, it ends, leaving it up to us to decide what happens in the long run. Of course, we'd like to believe that, over time, her gracious charm wins him over and they live happily ever after. But we don't know, do we?

For the moment, I'd like for us to look at what was happening in the story. Henry Higgins didn't know it, but in the hours, the days, the months he and Eliza were together, something was happening to him. She was becoming a part of him, an important part of him. And, although he was reluctant to admit it, when she left, it was a part he didn't want to lose.

I've said it again and again: we become a part of that with which we associate on a continual basis. Eliza learned about proper English from all the associations in the Higgins household. And she learned good manners and charm, Oh, not from the Professor, but from his mother and from the Colonel. And, I dare say, something good began to happen to Higgins during the times he was with Eliza.

It's true. We tend to become like that with which we associate on a continual basis. That means we can decide who we want to become and begin to shape our lives in that way by the choices we make about the people we associate with and by the habits by which we live.

I am so grateful that God has placed some wonderful people along my path in life. They are people with brilliant minds, people with warm and loving hearts, and people who worked hard and lived their lives with competence and integrity. I have been wise enough to recognize their excellence and I have wanted to be like them. So, when I was in their presence I have breathed deeply, trying to catch something of their spirit. And, I am convinced that most of what is good in my life is because God has reached out to me through such people. Their influence upon my life is beyond expression.

By the same token, if I had chosen to spend most of my time with those who took lower roads, my life would have gone in another direction, I am sure. But, I chose to embrace the influence of my parents, my teachers, my pastors, my friends, those whose lives called forth the best from me. And today, my life bears their imprint upon me for good. I am glad that I grew accustomed to so many of the right people!

Right people, and right behaviors. Someone has said, "You are what you do." There is a lot of truth in that. The things we do day in and day out have a way of shaping us in good or bad ways. I take regular baths, I brush my teeth, I eat three meals a day, and I say, "Thank you" and "Please." I turn out the lights when I leave a room. I live within my income. I say my prayers. I read the Bible. I go to worship every week. I do those things because I have always done them. They are habits and they have shaped my life in good ways. Don't ever underestimate the power of habitual behavior. We do tend to become like that with which we associate on a continual basis. So, we can decide who we want to be, decide what associations and what behaviors will help us to become that person, then commit ourselves to those associations and to those behaviors on a daily basis. Those experiences will go a long way in shaping who we become.

That's why Paul wrote to his beloved church at Philippi, "Whatever is true, whatever is honorable, whatever is just, whatever is pure, whatever is pleasing, whatever is commendable, if there is any excellence and if there is anything worthy of praise, think about those things, and the God of peace will be with you." It is a choice, you know. Paul was saying, "Choose to fill your mind and heart and life with good things, then God's peace, God's fullness, God's completeness will be yours."

The Church has understood that for centuries. That's why, throughout our history, we have stressed what we have called, "holy habits". There are good things you do, not just when you feel like it and not just when your faith is strong and your inclination leads in that direction. You do them regularly, habitually, and as a matter of commitment, because they shape our lives in good ways. Among the holy habits are prayer, the reading of scripture, associating with people of faith, acts of Christian compassion, and worship and the sacraments. Don't underestimate the power of those experiences to shape your life in good ways if you do them day after day, month after month, year after year, throughout our lives. They become a part of us, and we become like them.

I think about the man who said that he put his faith in a drawer for safe keeping, while he gave primary attention to other areas of his life. When, several years later, he returned for it, his faith was not there. It had died for lack of the daily nurture and support so essential to the life of faith. He had become like the things to which he *had* given priority. Professor Higgins sang, "I've grown accustomed to her face." Well, isn't it obvious? You can't become accustomed to something that is occasional, hit and miss, on again off again. No, you become accustomed only to that which is a custom, that which is a habit. The right habits can profoundly shape our lives.

The Cherokee Tribe of Native Americans has a story which says it. An elder was teaching his grandchildren about life. He said, "A fight is going on inside of me. It is a terrible fight and it is between two wolves. One wolf represents fear, anger, greed, arrogance, and lies. The other wolf stands for joy, peace, love, hope, kindness, generosity, truth, and faith. This same fight is going inside you, and inside every other person too." The children thought about that for a few moments, then one of them asked, "Grandfather, which wolf will win?" The old Cherokee replied, "The one you feed."

Prayer: Loving Father, save us from associations and behaviors that drag us down and dull the divine image in us. Call us anew to those daily habits that inspire us and call forth the best from within us, as Jesus does, in whose name we pray. Amen.

Where Is Love?

I Corinthians 13:1-8a; I John 4:7-12, 19

The musical, "Oliver," is about a little orphan boy named Oliver Twist who had a very difficult life. His mother had been unmarried and pregnant, although her family had not known she was pregnant. In shame, she ran away from home and went to a state run work house. The sign outside said: "Work House – Home for Paupers and Orphans." There she gave birth to her child and shortly thereafter, she died. So, that is where Oliver Twist spent his early years.

The work there was hard and the discipline severe. The conditions were stark and harsh. The ones in charge were a Mr. Brumble and his wife. They, and the Board of Governors, ate sumptuously, while the orphans were fed gruel, and always too little of it at that. So, there they were: institutionalized orphans who were worked hard and fed little. They were always hungry. In fact, the musical opens with a production number in which all of the children were dreaming and singing about "food, glorious food."

One day, after the sparse meal was consumed, the boys at Oliver's table drew straws to see which of them would seek a second helping. Of course, Oliver lost, so he was to be the one. With great trepidation, he got up from his seat and approached the intimidating, authoritarian couple. Extending his bowl, Oliver said, timidly, "Please sir, I want some more." Mr. Brumble exploded in anger: "More!" he said. "You want more!" Then, taking Oliver by the ear and leading him from the room, he began to sing, "Never before has a boy wanted more!" Of course, he was wrong. They had always wanted more. They just had been afraid to ask. Can you imagine what it is like to live in such circumstances, always being tired and hungry, but always too afraid to say anything? Well, Oliver said something, and he got into trouble because of it.

As punishment, Mr. Brumble decided to sell Oliver into servitude. With Oliver in tow, he walked down the street singing, "Boy for sale. He's yours to keep." A few inquired about the price and then turned away, so Brumble kept lowering the asking price. Get that now, a child unwanted and discounted in value. Finally, at a lowered price, he was bought by an undertaker, who wanted him as a laborer and as a coffin follower. He was to be a part of the funeral scene, pretending grief. But the undertaker insisted upon a conditional sale. If it didn't work out, he could return Oliver for a full refund. As the story unfolds, an older boy in the undertaker's house had some harsh things to say about Oliver's mother. They got into a fight, Mr. Brumble was called, and Oliver was returned to the home for paupers and orphans. Oliver was put into solitary confinement, in a basement room with bars on the windows.

Just look at what Oliver had experienced in his brief life: worked too hard; fed too little; offered for sale; discounted in value; passed from person to person. And now he was locked in a room all by himself, and no one in all the world seemed to know or care. What he wanted more than anything was to be loved, but that was something he had never experienced. He began to sing. It was a questioning song. Let's listen...

"Where is love? Does it fall from skies above? Is it underneath the willow tree that I've been thinking of?
Where is she who I close my eyes to see? Will I ever know the sweet 'hello' that's meant for only me?
Who can see where she may hide? Must I travel far and wide 'til I am beside the someone who I can mean something to? Where, where is love?
Every night I kneel and pray: let tomorrow be the day when I see the face of someone who I can mean something to. Where, where is love?"

The words of Oliver's song are important because they express the deepest longing of every human being. Every one of us longs to feel special, not lost in the crowd, not just cared about as a part of a large group. No, we long to feel singled out, cared about, and given gifts of love with our name on them. That's what Oliver was singing about: "Will I ever know the sweet 'hello' that's meant for only me." Do you hear it? Do you feel it, that need to feel special?

And, we need to feel loved. We need to know that there are those who care about what happens to us and who have our best interests at heart. We need to know that there are those who are so close to us that they feel along with us, laughing when we laugh, and crying when we cry. That is the universal human longing! Oliver sang about it: "Must I travel far and wide 'til I am beside the someone who I can mean something to?" Not only did he sing about it, he prayed for it: "Every night I kneel and pray: let tomorrow be the day when I see the face of someone who I can mean something to. Where is love?"

We all need it. We all want it. We all pray for it. The most basic need in life is to be loved. Recently I read about a young mother who was having the worst day of her life. The washing machine had broken down, the sink drain backed up, the telephone kept ringing with sales pitches, her head ached, and the mail carrier brought a bill she had no money to pay. Almost to the breaking point, she lifted her one year old into his high chair, leaned her head against the tray, and began to cry. Without a word, the baby took his pacifier out of his mouth and stuck it in his mother's mouth!

That's the way we want to be loved. We want someone to be so tuned in to us that they experience what we experience. They care. And they do whatever they can, even at great cost, to help. I say it again, the most basic need in life is to be loved. And that presents a problem: we want it so much that often we are taken in by that which claims to be love, but which in fact is something else. There are people in our lives who want to use us while claiming to love us. And, because we want so badly to be loved, often we are taken in by the counterfeit version.

The Oliver Twist story is a good example. There, in solitary confinement, after he had finished his song, he was leaning against the bars of the window. They gave way, and he escaped. He made his way to London, alone, hungry, penniless, and friendless. In London, he met and was befriended by a slightly older boy named Jack Dawkins, but all his friends called him "the Artful Dodger." He took Oliver to a place where he and some other boys lived with and were guided by an older man named Fagin. It was a not a good environment. They smoked. They drank gin. They gambled. And they lived on the street by their wits, picking pockets, shoplifting from merchants, and stealing from the wealthy. The one who taught them how to do all of this was Fagin, who sang, "Money doesn't grow on trees, boys, you've got to pick a pocket or two." As I said, it was not a good environment. But, they had more food than Oliver had ever had. They looked after one another in a way. And, although they used Oliver more than they loved him, it was closer to love than anything he had ever experienced. So, at least for awhile, he was willing to settle for that.

I wonder how many of us settle for less than love. Let me tell you what love is. Paul writes, "Love is patient and kind. Love does not insist upon its own way." In other words, love does not *use* another person. It cares enough to do what is in the best interest of the loved one. That is how Oliver could have recognized the counterfeit caring. They were teaching each other to drink, lie, cheat, and steal. They fed him and housed him, that's true. But they did not love him in authentic ways, because love does not always do what I *want*, love does what I *need*. Underline that!

Were you struck, as I was, by the shallowness of the statement made by Woody Allen some time ago? Woody Allen and his former lover, Mia Farrow, had adopted a number of children. Among them was a teenager named Soon Yi Previn. Woody had been a father figure to her, but he abused that relationship by having a sexual relationship with her. When asked about it, he said, "Love wants what it wants." Can you believe he said that? "Love wants what it wants." No, Woody, that's not love. Selfishness wants what it wants. Love wants what is best for the one who is loved, even at great personal costs. As Paul wrote, "Love does not insist upon its own way."

When you love someone, you don't just do what you want. But there is more to it than that. Listen carefully: nor do you always do what the loved one wants! Where is it written that if you love someone you always do what they want? When love has grown up to maturity, you don't always do what they want. You do what they need: we listen, we care, we try to respond with sensitivity, but finally, we don't just give what is asked for. We give what is best.

There are few things parents and grandparents need to hear more than that. I have so many parents say to me, "Jim, I love my children so much that I can't say 'No' to them." Well, if that is love, it is misguided love. Wise, strong love does not just give what is asked. I suggest to you that when we simply give what is asked without thinking of what is best, it is not because we love them so much. Rather, it is because we want them to love us, and we are afraid that if we say, "No", they will not love us any more. Don't you see, that really is selfishness. It is more concerned with being loved than with loving. The wisest, strongest love does what is in the best interest of the one who is loved, even if they hate us for it!

Do you want to know how to recognize real love? It is more than good feelings. Our culture has been captured by feelings. We like to feel good. We like to make others feel good. So, too many of us confuse love with good feelings. They are not the same. Here is the test: real love, strong love, wise love calls forth the best from the one who is loved. I don't care how it feels, if what you are experiencing does not help the other person to be the best person he or she can be, it is not real love. Elizabeth Barrett Browning helped me to recognize that. She wrote of her love for Robert by saying, "I love you not only for what you are, but for what I am when I am with you." Isn't that beautiful? Love calls forth the best from within us.

When Oliver Twist was with the Artful Dodger and Fagin and his band of petty thieves, it felt better than anything he had ever experienced. But their actions were not helping Oliver to be the best Oliver. So, no matter how it felt, it was not love. There is not time or space to tell the entire story, but at the end of the musical, Oliver was reunited with his real family. The family had always thought that Oliver's mother had run away from home because she was jilted by her boyfriend. They never knew that she was pregnant and had had a child. His mother's uncle, now Oliver's great uncle, a man of some wealth and influence, found Oliver, took him in, and raised him as his own. There, in his family's care, Oliver had a room of his own, plenty of food to eat, books to read, and schools to attend. He felt safe and secure, and, most important of all, he felt special. There were people who cared enough to do what was best for him. For the first time in his life, he knew that he was genuinely loved.

Would you like to be loved like that? Would you like to be able to love like that? Well, that is what the Christian gospel is about. The passage from I John says, "God's love was revealed among us in this way: God sent his only son into the world so that we might live through him." That is where it all begins. God loves us with a love which is unconditional, a love that never gives up on us, a love that gives life. God loves us, and once that love is at work in us, it helps us become the kinds of persons who can pass it on and love others in that same life-giving way. As I John goes on to say, "We love because he first loved us." So, we are loved and then we love. We receive and then we pass it on. And I'm here to tell you that you cannot pass on that which you have not received. If you want to be able to love in a healthy and life-giving way, you must first *be* loved. You must say "yes" to that love that comes to us from God.

And, that love which God gives to us through Christ meets all the criteria I have already named. It gives us not so much what we want, but what we need. Who wanted a baby in a manger? Who wanted an itinerant carpenter and teacher? Who wanted a death on a cross followed by a resurrection? The answer is, no-one. No-one was asking for that. If you ask us what we want, and if we are honest, we might say, "How about a sizable account in my name in a Swiss bank? How about that?" No, God does not give us what we think we want, but what we need. And what He gives calls forth the best from within us. What He gives helps us to become the best we can be. And He gives it to us even if we hate Him for it, even if we crucify Him because of it. Because what we need is to be loved by a Savior!

And, here is the key. The keystone of the Christian gospel is there at the cross. It is there in the suffering love we experience at the cross. Jesus said, "Greater love has no one than this, that he lay down his life for his friends." I came to this understanding late in my life, but that is how you can tell whether or not someone loves you. And, it is how you can tell how much you love someone else: not just by what is said, not just by the goose bumps that are stirred up, not even by what is done when it is easy or convenient or inexpensive. Anyone can love like that. The question is, are you or they willing to suffer, if need be, on behalf of the one who is loved? Real love and vulnerability are inseparable. When you love you become vulnerable to hurt. So, the willingness to endure that, the willingness to continue in that is the essence of love. There at the cross we experience the great heart of God. Authentic love is willing to suffer for the one who is loved!

I said earlier, that when he was reunited with his family, Oliver Twist experienced love for the first time in his life. That is not entirely true. There was a girl. She had grown up among the gang of petty thieves and she was one of them. But somewhere along the way she had learned to love, but not the kind of counterfeit love that takes and manipulates and uses in the name of love. No, she had learned to love with a giving kind of love, a love that does not count the cost. She saw what the gang was doing to Oliver, so she tried to steal him away from the gang so he could be reunited with his family. And, in that effort, she lost her own life. That's love. Greater love has no one than this, that you lay down your life for your friends.

Would you like to be loved like that? Would you like to be able to love like that? Well, the place to start is by trusting God and all that God has taught us in the Christian gospel. Listen: whoever you are, whatever you have been or done, you are loved by God. You are a child of God, loved and cherished and provided for by Him. You are of infinite worth, worth even Jesus' death upon the cross. Believe that. Trust that. Begin to live your life as if you trust that. You receive that kind of love from God and then you pass it on. You love others in the same way that God has loved you. That's the way it works. "We love, because He first loved us."

Where is love? It's there!

Prayer: God, our Father, we are grateful beyond words that You love us. You love us wisely, strongly, unconditionally. We are grateful that You give us not always what we want, but what we need. You love us in a way that calls forth the best from within us. You love us even at great cost, even the death of Your Son. Help us now to believe in Your love, to trust in it, so that we can receive it. And then, having received it, and having allowed it to nourish us, help us to pass it on, so that it can do for others what it has done for us. We pray now in gratitude for Your amazing love. Amen.

Consider Yourself At Home

Ephesians 2:8-20

The musical, "Oliver," is about Oliver Twist, an orphan boy who was born in a state run work house, a home for paupers and orphans. He spent the early years of his life there. He was not treated very well there. He, along with the other children, were worked hard and fed little. And, when they were punished, they were punished severely.

Oliver was sold into servitude, as we noted in the last chapter, then taken back to the work house when that didn't work out well. He was then put into solitary confinement. He was pretty much alone in the world, without any family that he knew about, and without any close friends. In his entire life he had never felt special or cared about. In the previous chapter we remembered the time, in one of his lower moments, when he sang a questioning song, "Where is love?" He had heard about love, but he had never experienced it.

Fortunately, he was able to escape from the work house. He made his way to London, alone, hungry, penniless, and friendless. There he was befriended by an older boy, Jack Dawkins, known to his buddies as "the Artful Dodger." The two of them hit it off and Jack invited Oliver to join with him and the adult leader, Fagin, and his band of petty thieves. He invited Oliver to share their lodging, their food, and indeed to share everything they had. He invited Oliver to become one of them. This is how he expressed it. Let's listen:

"Consider yourself at home, consider yourself part of
the family.
We've taken to you so strong it's clear we're going to
get along.
Consider yourself well in, consider yourself part of the
furniture.
There isn't a lot to spare, who cares, whatever we've
got we share.
If it should chance to be we should see some harder
days,
Empty larder days, why grouse? Always a chance we'll
meet
Somebody to foot the bill, then the drinks are on the
house!
Consider yourself our mate, we don't want to have no
fuss,
For after some consideration we can state: consider
yourself one of us!"

Consider yourself at home? Oliver had never had a home. Consider
yourself part of the family? Oliver had never been part of a family.
Consider yourself one of us? Oliver had never been wanted or welcomed
anywhere in his entire life. And, it felt good, so very good. Someone
wanted him. Someone cared about him. That felt good!

It always feels good to belong to a group. I remember the good
feelings stirred up by the "Cheers" jingle: "Sometimes you want to go
where everybody knows your name, and they're always glad you came."
That feels good!

I said in the previous chapter that the most basic need in life is to
be loved. Very close to that is a second basic need, and that is the need
to belong. Every human being needs to belong to a group with a shared
vision, with shared values, and with a shared commitment to care about
and support one another. Clearly, it is not God's intention for us to live
our lives in loneliness and isolation. That is why He has placed a longing
within us to belong. And, that is why He has placed us in families, and
called us into the faith community which is the church. To belong to
such a group is a basic need in life.

Of course, not just any group will do. Being part of a gang or a mob might *feel* good but not *be* good. The group Oliver joined in London did not meet the criteria for love that I gave in the previous chapter. Healthy groups give us not always what we *want*, but what we *need*. Healthy groups bring out the best in us. Those are the kinds of groups we need, and we do need to belong to them, because God did not create us for solitary life.

So many people misunderstand that. In fact, our entire culture seems to negate that. We place such a premium on rugged individualism, independence and self-reliance that the importance of community is downgraded. Even much popular religion is individualistic in its emphasis. So much of what I read and hear seems to be saying that to be Christian is simply to have a personal relationship with the God made known in Christ. It's just one on One, you and God. But that is not Biblical religion. The Bible knows nothing of isolated, individualistic religion. From beginning to end in the Bible, if you belong to God you also belong to a faith community. You belong either to the people of Israel in the Old Covenant, or to the church in the New Covenant. Clearly, if you belong to God, you also belong to all of the other people who belong to God. It's a group experience, and it's a package deal.

The scripture from Ephesians is addressed to Gentile Christians who had been outside the Jewish community of faith. Paul said, "Once you were aliens and strangers" outside the community of faith. But now, In Christ, you who once were far off have been brought near. You are no longer aliens and strangers. The dividing wall of hostility has been broken down. You belong! You are part of the family!

That is one of the things that impressed me about Big Canoe Chapel, the last congregation I served before retirement. The people in that congregation come from a variety of faith traditions, but in that congregation we were one family. We said, we don't want you to abandon your faith tradition when you become a member of the Chapel. We want you to bring your faith tradition with you. People did, and, we were enriched by our differences. I have often said that the truth is not given to any one part of the Body of Christ. That is one reason we need one another. We can learn from one another. We can grow as we share together. I like the quote: "One of my most important gifts to you is my difference from you." We learn from one another, and one of the most important things we learn is that we do not have to think the same in order to love the same!

I will never forget my first experience in leading a Disciple Bible study. We had a variety of people in that group. We were intentional about it. We had people from many different faith traditions and people with a variety of theologies. And, for awhile, we really went at it, each person contending for his or her point of view. But, over time, we came to love one another. And we discovered something important. Listen carefully now, because I'm about to say something important: we discovered that it's okay to put our beliefs together in our minds in different ways; it's okay to use different language to talk about our faith. That is okay, because what is far more important is that we had shared a common experience of God's grace. By grace, we all belong to Him. And, because we belong to Him, we also belong to one another. That means that what unites us is far stronger and more important than what might otherwise separate us!

We need one another in our diversity. That is why I like to call myself a Cathobaptoorthometholupentepalianpresbygationalist! I want to embrace and to be embraced by the entire Body of Christ!

There is a richness in our diversity, but a danger too. I remember saying to someone that a diverse congregation is a lot like marriage. In marriage we are attracted to our opposite. Instinctively we are drawn to someone unlike us. We need for them not to duplicate us, but to complement us. We need someone unlike us, but as soon as are married, too often we begin trying to change them to make them just like us. Of course, you can't change another person. But, if you could, you would destroy the very reason you were attracted to them in the beginning.

No, there is a richness in our Christian diversity. We can learn from one another and have our lives enlarged by one another. But we must resist the temptation to invalidate one another and to try to make everyone just like us. Remember: "One of my most important gifts to you is my difference from you." Years ago, John Wesley said, "May we not all be of one heart, even though we are not all of one opinion? Herein may all the children of God unite." That is the source of our oneness: we all belong to one another because we all belong to the same God.

When we are what we are supposed to be in God's family, the church, we welcome everyone. We care about everyone. Everyone has a name and a place. We share our lives together, rejoicing with those who rejoice and weeping with those who weep. And, in whatever ways we can, we extend a helping hand. Everyone needs to be a part of a group like that. One of my favorite images of the church is that of a group of children sitting on a curb, crying. An adult came along and asked, "What are you crying about?" A little girl sniffed, "We have a pain in Billy's stomach." That's the church at its best!

I was only seven years old when I made a faith commitment and became a member of the church. I remember that experience vividly. I made my public expression of faith, members of the congregation came down to the front of the sanctuary to welcome me, and I cried. I cried tears of joy, because it felt so good to belong!

The need to belong is basic. And, it is instinctive. When we experience something joyful, or receive good news, there is something about us that needs to share it. We don't want to keep it to ourselves, do we? And, when we experience disappointment or sorrow, we also seek out a community for sharing. And, throughout the world, people have not only gathered with others, we have even developed rituals with which to express our deep feelings in community.

Whether in family, or church, or town, we instinctively find ways to ritualize our deepest life experiences. In every culture and in every religion we have done it. We ritualize birth, birthdays, graduations, marriage, anniversaries, promotions, retirement, and death. And, we declare holidays to ritualize the significant events of our shared past. We do all of that because we need to do it. We need to do it with others.

Recently I was reading an account by Tom Long about the night he was staying in a motel in a large city. Beside the elevator was a sign that said, "Party tonight! Room 210, 8:00 p.m. Everyone invited!" Later the sign came down, replaced by another sign that said the first had been a hoax, a practical joke played on all the sales reps, the vacationing families, and the curious motel employees who read it. In thinking about that experience, Long wrote: "That it was a hoax made sense, of course, but in a way it was too bad. For a brief moment, those of us staying at the motel were tantalized by the possibility that there might just be a party going on somewhere to which we were all invited – a party where it didn't make much difference who we were, when we walked in the door, or what motivated us to come; a party we could come to out of boredom, loneliness, curiosity, responsibility, eagerness to be in fellowship, or simply out of a desire to come and see what was happening; a party where it didn't matter nearly as much what got us in the door, as what would happen to us after we arrived." Then Long concluded: "Perhaps if there is to be such a party, the church is going to have to throw it."

You know what? I think that's exactly what the church is supposed to be: the one place in all the world where everyone who walks through the door is welcome, no matter what his or her reason for being there, a place where mercy and grace are abundant and joy is obvious, and a place where lonely hearts find fellowship and broken hearts find healing.

Let's let the Artful Dodger issue the invitation to that kind of church to us all: "Consider yourself at home. Consider yourself part of the family. Consider yourself one of us!" Welcome to God's church. You belong here!

Prayer: Father, we do want to belong. More than that, we *need* to belong. But save us from letting our need lead us to disingenuous groups and counterfeit love. Lead us to real community in which we are loved with a love that is unconditional, that gives what we really need and which brings out the best in us. We pray in the name of Jesus, the Lord of the church. Amen.

The Hills Are Alive With the Sound of Music

Matthew 13:16-18; Isaiah 40:13

"The Sound of Music" opened on Broadway in November of 1959. It was an extraordinary success, running for 1,443 performances and winning eight Tony Awards. It was made into a movie, starring Julie Andrews and Christopher Plummer, which opened in New York in March of 1965. The movie won five Academy Awards, including one for best picture. It set box office records and became the most successful movie musical of all time. I have friends who have loved it so much that they have seen the movie ten or twelve times. There is something about the story and the music that captivates us, and sends us out humming the tunes and singing the songs.

The musical is about a young postulate named Maria, preparing to become a nun, in the Abbey at Salzburg, Austria. Maria tries to follow the rules and regimentation of the Abbey, but with less than perfect success. The mother abbess, in charge of the abbey, suspects that Maria is not ready to take her final vows. So, she decides to send her out into the world to find herself, and to determine the course her life should take.

Maria is asked to become the governess for a family of seven children, ranging in age from three to sixteen. They are the children of Captain Georg von Trapp, a wealthy, retired Captain in the Austrian navy. He had lost his wife to illness some time before and was still in grief. Because of his grief, and because of his military orientation, he was trying to run his household with the discipline he used as Captain of a ship. He kept his children at arm's length, and insisted that their governess manage them with the same discipline and regimentation. They wore uniforms, and they were to come when summoned by a ship's whistle. They were not to play; they were to get their exercise by marching. And, there was to be no singing either, even though before their mother's death, music had been an important part of the von Trapp household. It is not surprising, then, that the children expressed their displeasure by making life miserable for a succession of governesses. The last one had stayed only two hours! You get the picture: discipline was a substitute for displays of affection, and there was to be no playing, no laughing, no singing, and no joy. It was into that not so promising setting that Maria was sent.

What had she done to deserve that? Well, at the abbey, Maria was "different." I'll talk a bit more about that in the next chapter. But, she did not act like the other nuns. She marched to the beat of a different drummer. And, consequently, many of the sisters at the abbey saw Maria not as a gift, but as a problem. They sang, "Maria's not an asset to the abbey!"

People who are "different" do not easily conform. They don't fit in very readily. You see, Maria saw things that others did not see. She heard things that others did not hear. There they were in the midst of the magnificent Austrian Alps. The beauty was breathtaking, if you could see it. Maria would look out from the cloistered walls of the abbey, see the beauty, and she would hear the mountains calling to her. She answered that call, and went running up into those hills. And that's where the musical begins, with Maria caught up in the wonder of it all. She runs, she jumps, she dances, and she sings. Oh, how she sings! Let's listen:

"The hills are alive with the sound of music,
With songs they have sung for a thousand years;
The hills fill my heart with the sound of music,
My heart wants to sing every song it hears.
I go to the hills when my heart is lonely,
I know I will hear what I've heard before;
My heart will be blessed with the sound of music,
And I'll sing once more."

Maria is so caught up in the beauty and wonder of this wonderful world that she forgets the time and stays longer than she should, missing evening vespers. Her absence is noted at the abbey, and one of the nuns reports her absence to the mother abbess. "I can't find Maria anywhere," she says. "I've looked in all the usual places." Mother replies, "Considering it's Maria, I suggest you look in all the *unusual* places!"

Just at that moment, Maria comes running, breathlessly, into the abbey, and there they are: the mother abbess and a group of nuns, talking abut the problem that is Maria. The mother abbess summons Maria to her office. Maria is apologetic. She is genuinely repentant. "But," she says, "the hills call to me." Mother asks, "Maria, what is the most important thing you have learned here?" Immediately, Maria says, "To find out what is the will of God and to do it wholeheartedly." That answer is right, of course. So, the mother abbess sends Maria out of the abbey, into the world, to search for God's will in her life. And that is how she became governess to the seven von Trapp children.

I said earlier that Maria saw things that others did not see. She heard things that others did not hear. That's because Maria did not limit herself to seeing with her eyes and hearing with her ears. She looked and listened with her heart as well. And, when any of us do that, a whole new world of meaning is opened to us. When Maria heard the hills singing, she began to sing in response. She sang, "The hills fill my heart with the sound of music, my heart wants to sing every song it hears!" When Maria heard the music and when she saw the beauty around her, her heart became more beautiful as well. And, as a result, she was able to share that beauty and that joy with others.

Because she could see, Maria was able to see past the mischievous acts of the von Trapp children, even the frog put in her pocket and the rumors of spiders in her bed. She saw that they were not really bad children, as the previous governesses had thought. Really, they were just sad, needing some attention, needing some fun in their lives, and above all, needing love. And, as for the captain, though the early encounters between Maria and the captain were contentious, Maria was able to see that the captain was really grieving and lonely. His insistence upon discipline was only a cover for his own pain and loneliness. There was an early battle of wills. When Maria refused to be intimidated by the captain's brusque manner, he asked, "Were you this much trouble at the abbey?" Maria replied, "O, much more sir!"

In the days that followed, Maria won the children's trust and affection. She discarded the uniforms and made play clothes for them, and they began to play. They hiked, and they biked, and they paddled canoes all over that beautiful country. And, she taught them to sing. Remember, "Doe, a deer, a female deer; Ray, a drop of golden sun; Me, a name I call myself; Far, a long, long way to run; Sew, a needle pulling thread; La, a note to follow sew; Tea, a drink with jam and bread, that will bring us back to doe." There is a great line in that song, "When you know the notes to sing, you can sing most anything." Come to think of it, I could do a chapter on that song as well! Once you get the basics down in life, you can apply them everywhere, and those basic truths can enliven every moment of every day. Once you learn the notes…

But, I digress. Maria and the children begin to sing. In fact, they sing everywhere!

For the first time in months, there was laughter and singing in the von Trapp household. After returning from a trip, the captain heard singing in the house. He followed the sound, only to discover that it was his children singing, "The hills are alive with the sound of music." He joined in the singing. And, afterwards, there was hugging all around.

And, that was the start of it. The captain's hard heart began to melt. He began getting to know his children, and loving them. And, though he did not yet know it, he began to fall in love with Maria. So much of that happened because of Maria's unique way of seeing, and because her joy in living was so contagious!

That's enough of the story for this chapter. We'll pick it up again in the next chapter. But for now, I would like to focus on something I said earlier. I said that Maria was able to see things that others did not see. She was able to hear things that others did not hear. She looked and listened not only with her eyes and ears, but also with her heart. Well, that is what the two scriptures I cited at the beginning of this chapter are about.

In the scripture from Matthew, Jesus is talking with his disciples. He says, "Blessed are your eyes for they see, and your ears, for they hear. Truly I tell you, many prophets and righteous people longed to see what you see, but did not see it, and to hear what you hear, but did not hear it." That ability to see and hear beyond the obvious is an important part of the life of faith.

In the scripture from Isaiah, the prophet is talking about the Jewish people there in Babylonian captivity. He is assuring them that they have not been forsaken, that God has heard their prayers and that He will end their captivity and allow them to return to Jerusalem. There is such joy in this news that Isaiah talks about the heavens singing in gladness, the earth erupting in celebration, and even the mountains singing for joy. That is in the Bible, but it sounds a lot like the song from "The Sound of Music," doesn't it? "The hills are alive with the sound of music." There it is, all around us, even there in that distant land of captivity: celebration, joy, and singing. But not everyone can sense it. Most would respond by saying, "Where? I don't see anything. I don't hear anything." How sad.

That is a major difference between a person of faith and the average person among us. Faith is not just believing in God. And, faith is not just having a trusting relationship with God, although that is essential. Faith is also perception, the ability to hear the voice of God when He is speaking. Faith is the ability to see the hand of God at work in all the common, ordinary events of daily life. Faith as perception.

Let me tell you about some people in the Bible who had that kind of faith. Thousands of years ago, there was a man out tending his father-in-law's sheep. He saw a bush that appeared to be on fire, and he turned aside to examine it more closely. As he approached the bush, he heard a voice saying, "Don't come near. Take off your shoes, for the ground on which you are standing is holy ground." God used that event to turn Moses' life around. Moses was changed from an ordinary sheep herder into Moses, the law giver, Moses the deliverer, Moses the most towering figure in the Hebrew Bible. Do you know what I think? I think the average among us would have passed by that bush without seeing anything out of the ordinary. But it was a turning point in Moses' life, because he could see and hear.

There was another man. His name was Jacob, and he was a liar and a cheat. You remember that he stole his brother's birthright and then ran away in fear. He ran and ran until he fell down, exhausted, in the wilderness and there he went to sleep. In his sleep he had an encounter with God that changed his life. When he awoke, he said, "Surely the Lord is in this place, and I didn't even know it." He called the place, "Bethel" which, in Hebrew, means "the house of God." Again, do you know what I think? I think most people would have spent the night in that wilderness and found nothing more than a wilderness. But Jacob's life was changed there because he could see and hear.

The same thing happens every Sunday in worship. Two people are sitting side by side in the sanctuary: one is planning Monday's agenda; the other has a life-changing encounter with God. And why not? Because wherever you are at any given moment, it is Bethel, the house of God; that is, when you can see and hear.

Unfortunately, most of us have been conditioned to look for God only in special places, and to listen for God only in certain circumstances. We look and listen only in those "stained glass" parts of life. But, of course, God is bigger than that. He goes wherever He pleases; he speaks however he chooses. While in college, I heard Dr. Carl Michalson say something that stayed with me. He said, "Jesus of Nazareth came into the world to do away with religion." What?, I thought. I always thought Jesus came to start a new religion, Christianity. For days I thought about what he had said, I wrestled with it, lost sleep over it, and then it hit me. Of course! What he was saying was that Jesus came into the world to do away with religion as a separate category of life. There is not religion over here and the rest of life over there. No! There is just life, and God is the God of the whole thing, and God is at work in the whole thing. And, if we look and listen only in those "stained glass" parts of life, we are going to miss most of what God is doing! If we look for God only in the expected places, we will miss Him when He reaches out to us through a burning bush, in a wilderness camp site, a manger in a stable, or songs up in the hills.

When you listen for the voice of God, what do you listen for? Do you listen for the kind of voice you can record on a recording device? Well, if that is what you are listening for, you will have a long wait, I expect. I don't think that is the way God does it. No, the still, small voice the Bible talks about is more the sense of a presence, not ourselves, but Someone. It is a sense of well being, closely akin to the experience of being held. Perhaps we are impressed with a sense of "oughtness": we ought to do this or we ought not do that. Maybe we have been struggling with something and suddenly there is clarity. Perhaps someone or something pops into our mind, something we hadn't been thinking about, a thought seemingly out of nowhere. Perhaps there is a sudden infusion of strength, or courage, or hope. Something like that, I believe, is the voice of God. I know that God speaks to me, and that is the way He does it.

Well then, what I am saying is that if we want to see the hand of God at work, if we want to hear the voice of God, then we must look everywhere. We must listen to everything. We must put our antenna up and consider the possibility that, wherever we are, in every moment of every day, God is there, and God is at work!

Of course, when we do that, when we begin to look everywhere and listen to everything, how are we to know when it is God? Listen carefully, because this is the key: if it looks and sounds like Jesus, then we can know that God is there, at work. And, we can take off our shoes, because we are standing on holy ground!

So, if you want to know how to recognize God, the thing to do is to get to know Jesus. Christians believe that in Jesus we see God most clearly. So, walk with Jesus through the pages of the gospels. Live with him, listen to him, and get to know him. Focus your eyes with the spirit of Jesus. Tune your ears with the spirit of Jesus. Shape your heart by the heart of Jesus. Then, look at all of life and listen to all of life. And, whenever something looks and sounds like Jesus, you will know that God is there!

Once you begin to do that, do you know what will happen? You will be amazed! You will discover that God is all around you, seeking to make Himself and His will known to you, often in unexpected ways. And, once you begin to see and hear with faith, you will find yourself bumping into God at every turn. You will be like Brother Lawrence in the kitchen of the monastery, who said that he had learned to experience God among the pots and pans of the kitchen just as surely as his brothers did in the blessed sacrament.

Someone wrote about "finding love letters from God dropped daily in the streets." Have you experienced that? Well, they are there. God put them there, I'm sure of that. But you will never receive them unless you can see and hear. That is what Elizabeth Barrett Browning was saying,

> "Earth's crammed with heaven, and every common
>   bush afire with God,
> But only he who sees takes off his shoes; the rest sit
>   'round it and pick blackberries."

Let me underline it with this: an art gallery was celebrating the anniversary of its opening. As a part of the festivities, the owner borrowed some of the world's great art and put it on display. A woman walked though the gallery, glanced briefly at the art, then turned to the owner and said, with a dismissive wave of her hand, "I can't see what is so great about these paintings!" Immediately he replied, "No, madam, you can't. But don't you wish you could!"

"The hills are alive with the sound of music!" Can you hear it?

Prayer: Father, give us eyes with which to see You, and ears with which to hear You, then give us hearts responsive to all we see and hear. Make us come alive to all of life because we sense Your gracious presence everywhere. In the name of Jesus, who has made You known. Amen.

How Do You Solve a Problem Like Maria?

Psalms 8

As we learned in the previous chapter, "The Sound of Music" is about the young postulate named Maria, preparing to become a nun in the abbey at Salzburg, Austria. She has some difficulty following the rules and regimentation of the Abbey. So, the mother abbess, in charge of the abbey, suspects that Maria is not ready to take her final vows. She decides to send her out of the abbey into the world to find herself, and to determine the course her life should take.

That is how she became the governess for Captain Georg von Trapp. After the death of his wife, the captain tried to manage his household as if it were a ship, with the emphasis upon discipline and conformity. It's not surprising that the children had made life miserable for a succession of governesses.

As we learned in the previous chapter, Maria came into that unpromising situation and began to change things. Contrary to instructions, she exchanged the uniforms for play clothes. She taught the children to play and sing. And, when the captain heard the children singing, he joined in, there were hugs all around, and the sounds of music and laughter returned to von Trapp manor. It was Maria's joy, Maria's music, and Maria's vivaciousness that began to infect them all for good. It's instructive to know that, not only is disease contagious, health is contagious too. So, Maria began to infect the whole household with what it means to be fully and magnificently alive!

But, at least initially, she was not perceived in a positive way at the abbey. She was "different." Many of the nuns did not see her gifts or her capacity for contribution; they saw only her problems. I think back to the opening scenes of the movie which were some of the most beautiful, impressive scenes ever. There was Maria singing and dancing for joy in the magnificent Austrian Alps. I will never forget it: "The hills are alive with the sound of music."

As I have noted, Maria saw things that others did not see. She heard things others did not hear. Somehow, there in God's beautiful world, not only did she see the hills, the lakes, and the trees, she also saw God, and heard His call. The ability to hear the voice of God and the ability to see the hand of God at work in all the common events of daily life is one dimension I talked about in the previous chapter.

As she was seeing and listening there in the hills, she lost track of time, missed evening vespers, and rushed back to the abbey just as some of the nuns were talking about her. They were recounting her shortcomings. Let's listen:

> "She climbs a tree and scrapes her knee, her dress has
> got a tear,
> She waltzes on her way to Mass and whistles on the
> stair;
> And, underneath her wimple she has curlers in her
> hair,
> I even heard her singing in the abbey!
> She's always late for chapel but her penitence is real,
> She's always late for everything except for every meal;
> I hate to have to say it, but I very firmly feel
> Maria's not an asset to the abbey.
> How do you solve a problem like Maria?
> How do you catch a cloud and pin it down?
> How do you find a word that means Maria?
> A flibbertigibbet! A will-o'-the wisp! A clown!
> Many a thing you know you'd like to tell her,
> Many a thing she ought to understand,
> But how do you make her stay and listen to all you say,

How do you keep a wave upon the sand?
Oh, how do you solve a problem like Maria?
How do you hold a moonbeam in your hand?"

How do you solve a problem like Maria? Well, she did have some growing up to do. As long as she was at the abbey, it would have been nice to fit in a bit more comfortably with the routine. But, the biggest problem was not with Maria. The biggest problem was with the nuns who wanted everyone to be alike, to conform, to not get out of line; and, those who were different, unique, distinctive from the crowd, were seen as "problems." I wish they had known a quote that has become increasingly important to me. "There is no problem to be solved as important as a person to be loved." Read that again because it's important. I am glad that the mother abbess seemed to have a better grasp of the reality. The reality is that Maria is not a problem so much as she is a gift for all those who can see. She is the bright color in contrast with grayness. She is the song in contrast with noise. She is the excitement in contrast with dullness. Unpredictable, yes. Confusing, yes. Aggravating, sometimes. But dull and lifeless? Never! In short, I like her, and I'll bet God does too!

This is not a part of the story told in the musical, but I am sure that somewhere in her background, Maria had some influences which affirmed her, and taught her to love herself in healthy ways. You see, we can give to others only that which we have. So, clearly, Maria is able to give love and joy to the von Trapp family because someone had given it to her. Someone, somewhere, had taught her of her worth as a child of God. Someone, somewhere, had enabled her to love herself. Too often we distort Jesus' words and have him say, "Love your neighbor instead of yourself." But that is not what Jesus said. Jesus knew it before modern psychologists began to say it: we cannot love others in healthy, life-giving ways until we first learn to love ourselves. Where did we ever get the idea that we are not to love ourselves? Certainly not from Jesus. Listen: self love is not a problem. You can never love yourself too much. Certainly you can love yourself in unhealthy, inappropriate ways. But, self love is not a problem; self centeredness is the problem. Clearly, our lives are to be God centered; but once our lives are grounded in God centeredness, then we are able to love ourselves in right ways, and then to love others. We are able to do that because God first loved us. So, what Jesus said was, "Love your neighbor *as* you love yourself."

I remember something Father John Powell said: "Our lives are shaped by those who love us and by those who refuse to love us." That is true, isn't it? What if everyone in her life had dismissed her gifts and only noticed Maria's problems? What if she had had a steady diet of people telling her her faults and never her positive traits? She probably would have become a very different person, wouldn't she?

We all have scars from those people who did not love us as we needed loving. Perhaps a word here or there burned its way into our consciousness and became the way we see ourselves. You know those thoughtless words: "You're fat...you're not very smart...can't you do anything right?" I was told as a child just to say, "Sticks and stones may break my bones, but words can never hurt me." But that's a lie. Words do hurt. "Maria, you're a problem!" I'm glad she didn't believe that.

I read recently of a student who came home with two A's on his report card. His father criticized him because there were not three or more. Just down the street, another student came home with two A's on his report card. His father smiled, gave him a hug, and said, "I surely am glad you are my son!" Which of the two do you think was healthier, happier, and more of a joy to be around? "Our lives are shaped by those who love us, and by those who refuse to love us."

In case you don't know, I want you to know who you are. You are a child of God, created in His image. And, you are of infinite worth. I have always loved Psalms 8: "O Lord, how majestic is Your name in all the earth. When I look at Your heavens, the work of Your fingers, the moon and the stars that You have established; what are human beings that You are mindful of them, mortals that You care for them." So it would seem. We are tiny compared to the rest of creation. But listen, "And yet...and yet, You have made them a little lower than God, and crowned them with glory and honor." That's who you are, and don't ever forget it. Too often we say, "Well I'm...I'm only human". What do you mean *only* human? We haven't begun to take hold of the greatness of being human!

So, you are different? You are not like everyone else? Well, welcome to the human race! Every one of us is different. When God created us, he did not use human cookie cutters. Every one of us is a unique and unrepeatable miracle of God's creative power. Our "differentness" is not a problem, as the nuns at the abbey thought. Our "differentness" is our greatest gift! As I wrote in another chapter, "One of my most important gifts to you is my difference from you." I wish the nuns at the abbey had known that and were able to affirm that in Maria.

I like what one little fellow said. The sixth grade teacher asked the class, "What is here in the world today that was not here fifteen years ago?" She was expecting answers about inventions and innovations in technology. One little boy raised his hand and answered, "Me!" He was right! When he was created, something unique and wonderful entered the world.

Have you ever thought about how insulting it is to God to demean ourselves and to put ourselves down, as if somehow we were a mistake? Let me quote again from Father John Powell, as he scans the scriptures for the truth about us and then summarizes. He has God say, "There were other possible worlds I could have created. Yes, I could have made a world without you. But, don't you realize this, that I didn't want a world without you? A world without you would be incomplete for me. You are the child of my heart, the delight of my thoughts, the apple of my eye. Of course, I could have made you different: taller, shorter, born of different parents, born in a different place and into a different culture, endowed with a different set of gifts. But I didn't want a *different* you. It is *this* you that I love. Just as every grain of sand on the seashore and every snowflake that falls in wintertime has its own unique composition and structure, so are you composed and structured as no other human being has ever been. It is *this* you that I love, that I have always loved and will always love. If you should ever get down on yourself and feel that you are the type that only a mother could love, please remember this", and here Powell quotes scripture: "Even if a mother should forget the child of her womb, I will never forget you."

Do you hear that? Do you really hear that? You are a child of God, a unique, unrepeatable miracle. And, God loves you more than words can say. You are of infinite worth. That's who you are! It's true we don't always live like that, but that doesn't change who we are and what we are worth, it only gives us something to live up to.

In one of his books, my friend, Maxie Dunnam tells of the time his wife, Jerry, went on a retreat led by a nun, Sister Susan. But this nun was not like the ones at Maria's abbey. When Jerry returned from the retreat, she received a letter from Sister Susan, and enclosed with the letter was a prayer. In the prayer were these words, "O God, help me to believe the truth about myself, no matter how beautiful it is." Wow! How is that for a prayer?! God does not want to put us down, God wants to lift us up. God wants us to love ourselves and to believe in ourselves. Listen: our greatest sin in life may be our failure to embrace our true identity as a unique, one of a kind, cherished child of God!

I have struggled with it. As a young adult, I sometimes felt like a failure because I am not like my minister-father, or my minister-brother. My father was the only pastor I had until I went off to college, so he was the model, and I am not like him. Both my father and my brother were extroverted, take charge, at home in every crowd, back-slapping, "people people". I am much shyer, quieter, and less aggressive. Periodically, throughout my life, some people have said to me, "You don't act much like a preacher!" (Usually I have been inclined to respond, "Thank you!") But such statements have led me to wonder if I belonged. I am indebted to the woman who came up to me after a worship service, smiled, and said, "I think God knew what He was doing when He called you to preach!" God bless her! I needed to hear that. And, because of her and others like her, I am learning that I don't have to be like my father or my brother or like anyone else. It's okay to be me. In fact, it's good to be me. And, I want to pray, "O God, help me to believe the truth about myself, no matter how beautiful it is!"

When we read the story of creation, as it is written in the book of Genesis, we are told that God created the world and everything in it, then He stood back and looked at His creation and said, "It is good. It is very good!" Hey, that includes you. That includes me. God created you, the unique miracle of you, and God says you are good! Now, believe that. Live up to that. I pray that you too will believe that truth about yourself, no matter how beautiful it is!

Well, that is pretty much what I wanted to say in this chapter. When we are seeing clearly, we see that Maria was not so much a problem as she was a gift. I think most of the nuns finally came to see that too. And, it was only because she was able to feel loved and valued, and because she was able to love herself in a healthy way that she was able to bring love and joy and music to the von Trapp family. It is ever so: we love our neighbors as we love ourselves. And, we are able to love ourselves because God first loved us. That's in the Bible, you know.

Let me pull it all together and say it one more time. Fred Craddock, one of the great preachers of our time, tells of a baby born years ago in West Tennessee. The baby's mother was not married. Everyone in town knew, and life was tough for him during his growing up years. Some children were not allowed to play with him. People talked about him behind his back, and called him that ugly name. He felt left out, worthless, and lonely. For some reason, when he got to high school, he started going to church. People, by and large, were nice to him there, but he still felt self-conscious, so he stayed in the background. He would slip into a back pew just after the service started and he would slip out just before the benediction. He was afraid that someone would say, "What's a boy like you doing in church?"

One Sunday he waited too long to leave. He was caught up in the crowd, and before he could make his way through, he felt a hand on his shoulder. He turned to see who it was, and he froze in fear. It was the preacher! The preacher looked at his face for a long time, and the boy just knew he was trying to figure out who his father was. And he heard those words he had come to dread: "Whose boy are you anyway?" His whole body tensed. He wished he could disappear. But, before he could answer, the preacher broke into a smile and said, "I know who you are. I see the family resemblance. You're a child of God! Now you go out there and claim your inheritance!" In telling about it later, the boy said that that was the beginning of his life. He believed what the preacher said, and from that day on he saw himself in a different way, and acted like it. O, by the way, his name is Ben Hooper, and the people of Tennessee twice elected him governor.

Do you hear the good news in that? Maria, you're not a problem, you're God's gift to the world. And so are you, whoever you are. You are a child of God, created a little less than God Himself and crowned with glory and honor. That's who you are! Now, you believe that, and go out there and live like it!

Prayer: God, our Father, thank you for creating us and making us different, each of us one of a kind. Thank You for claiming us as Your children and for loving us just as we are. Now Father, help us, every one, to believe the truth about ourselves, no matter how beautiful it is. In Jesus' name we pray. Amen.

Climb Every Mountain

John 10:10; 8:12

As you have probably guessed by now, "The Sound of Music" is one of my favorite musicals. It is filled with upbeat, "sing-able" tunes. And, I admit, I'm a pushover for happy endings! I like it when love wins out and when goodness prevails.

When we first visited this musical I noted that the central character is Maria, a young postulate preparing to become a nun. We have learned a great deal about Maria in the last two chapters. To begin with, we saw her out there in the hills, singing and dancing, celebrating the joy of life. The song was, "The Hills Are Alive with the Sound of Music." I wrote about how Maria saw things others did not see and she heard things others did not hear. I noted that perception is an important part of faith: the ability to hear the voice of God, the ability to see the hand of God at work, even in the commonplace events of every day.

Then, in the previous chapter, we learned about Maria's problems at the abbey. Maria was "different," chafing under the rules and regimentation of the abbey. For example, she was late to prayer. In fact she was late for almost everything, except for meals. She whistled on the way to Mass. Occasionally she laughed out loud. And, several times she was even seen dancing! In the abbey no less! The older nuns at the abbey worried about her, singing, "How do you solve a problem like Maria?" But, I asserted that she was not a problem just because she was different. In fact, she was less a problem than she was a gift to the abbey, used by God to bring color, variety, and life to their community. And, remember the quote, "One of my most important gifts to you is my difference from you."

But, because of some of the difficulties, the mother abbess suspected that Maria was not ready to take her final vows as a nun. She sent her out of the abbey and into the world, to find herself and to find God's will for her life. That is how she became the governess to the seven von Trapp children. You remember that she quickly won the trust and then the love of the children. The captain began to lower his grief-induced defenses. He began getting to know his children, and to love them. So many good things were happening in their family because of Maria and because of the love and joy and vitality she brought to them.

And, in the process of all of that, Maria and Captain von Trapp began to fall in love. Maria didn't mean for it to happen. She didn't want it to happen. It just did. Perhaps she didn't even know it consciously, until she was confronted by the captain's fiancé. With perhaps not the best of motives, the baroness said that it was obvious to everyone. And, in her view, it was a bit unseemly for one preparing to become a nun to fall in love with a man, and he with her.

Maria was embarrassed, and frightened. So, without a word to anyone, she went running back to the abbey in fear. She went into seclusion, spending much of her time in prayer. She didn't quite know how to handle these new emotions. The mother abbess, a wise woman, summoned her. She pointed out that the abbey should not be used as a hiding place. She said that the life of faith is not a way of escaping from life, but as *the* way of embracing life and living it to the fullest. So, she sends Maria out of the abbey and back to the von Trapp home to search and to keep on searching until she finds her dream. She sings it. Let's listen:

> "Climb every mountain, search high and low,
> Follow every byway, every path you know.
> Climb every mountain, ford every stream,
> Follow every rainbow 'til you find your dream,
> A dream that will need all the love you can give,
> Every day of your life for as long as you live.

Climb every mountain, ford every stream,
Follow every rainbow 'til you find your dream."

Did you let the words of that song sink in? That song is about searching, and every human being does that. To be a human being is to be on a perpetual search for life at its best. Unfortunately, not everyone is as successful as Maria was in her search, but everyone I know is searching. We want to be happy. We want to be fulfilled. We want our lives to count for something. We don't want anything good to pass us by. We don't want to come to the end of our lives and feel that we have missed it. So, that is why we spend every day searching for what the mother abbess called "your dream".

As I observe life, I am impressed with the fact that only we human beings are searching. Every other creature in God's world is exactly what God created them to be. Only we human beings are free to be something other than what God intended. And, when we are not what we are created to be, we know it, don't we? There is that emptiness. There is that loneliness, that homesickness. There is that anxious restlessness. Augustine knew what he was talking about when he said, "Thou hast made us for Thyself, O God, and our hearts are restless 'til they find their rest in Thee."

Jesus said that that is the purpose of his coming into the world. He came to give us life, life spelled with a capital 'L", life which he called "abundant". He said it out loud: "I am the way." So, that is where we find our dream, and we won't find it anywhere else.

Jesus said it plain as day, as clear as can be. And yet, that is the very place most people refuse to look for their dream. I don't know what it is about us that makes us reluctant to see the obvious. For over two thousand years we have had the option of following Jesus, trusting Jesus, and making the God we meet in him the center of our lives. And, we have seen again and again what happens when we refuse to do that. We've done it and we have seen other people do it. We travel down one dead end street after another. We try this glittery thing and that glittery thing, only to discover that most of what glitters does not lead to light, but to darkness. Jesus said, "I am the light of the world." (Not *a* light, mind you, as if we have a number of valid options for our illumination.) No, Jesus says, "I am *the* light of the world. Whoever follows me will not walk in darkness, but will have the light of life." Jesus insists that it is in him that we will find our dream.

Years ago, G.K. Chesterton talked about people who spend their days searching for "cures that do not cure, blessings that do not bless, and solutions that do not solve." You would think we would learn!

I have often said to members of church staffs, "If what you are doing isn't working, change something!" Duh! If the way you are living your life isn't working very well, change it. If you haven't found your dream in the places you have been looking, why not look somewhere else? So many people insist upon looking for life in places where no-one has ever found it!

I remember the old vaudeville sketch made famous by Karl Valentin. The curtain opens upon a stage, empty except for a single street light, giving off a small circle of light. Valentin comes onto the stage and walks round and round in the circle of light as if searching for something. Soon a second man appears and joins in the search. He asks, "What did you lose?" Valentin replies, "The key. I lost the key." The two of them continue the search. Long minutes later, the second man asks, "Are you sure you lost it here?" "No," said Valentin, pointing to a dark corner of the stage, "I lost it over there." "Well, why are you looking here?" he asks. Valentin replies, "Because there is no light over there."

Dumb! Dumb! Looking in places it cannot possibly be found! I can't say it any clearer than that – it is a parable of contemporary life. Everyone is searching for meaning, for fulfillment, for love, for life, but most of the people I know are looking in all of the wrong places.

It's not that we do so many wrong things. In fact, most of the things we do are pretty good. In our search for the good life, we work, we spend time with our families, we go to classes, we pursue hobbies and recreation, we build houses and maintain them, we invest ourselves in our community, we go to worship. We do many good things. But, in the midst of our busyness, where is the thread that pulls it all together and gives meaning to the whole? What is the core reality that gives a sense of direction and the motivation and strength to pursue it? If you don't have that, it is pretty easy to mess up all the rest.

I like to remember that the word "holy" and the word "whole" come from the same root. That means that to be holy is to have all of life made whole, made whole because all the varied parts of life are gathered and organized around their proper center. And, for Christians, that proper center is God, the God made known in Jesus.

In the mother abbess song, she said that when we find our dream, that dream will need all the love we can give, every day of our life, for as long as we live. That is a good description of the life of faith. Once we discover that our dream for the good life, the abundant life, is fulfilled in God, we also discover that God requires all that we have to give. He asks for our first and best devotion. But, now hear me, that is not *instead of* our commitment to our families, or to our work, or to our recreation. No, He just asks for our highest allegiance, and then, as a result of that loyalty, all of the other important things in life are enhanced. We become a more loving family member, a more effective worker, and we discover that we are enjoying life more than ever before!

The scriptures declare, and I believe, that the fullest possible experience of life is to be found in Christ. When Jesus is Lord, life takes on a new, tangy flavor. There is an excitement, a meaning, a joy, which is available from no other source. Countless thousands of people throughout history have testified to it: in him is life! I like the way Alfred Lord Tennyson said it. Speaking of Jesus, he said, "He wakes in you desires you never can forget; he shows you stars you never saw before."

It's true. When I am in the company of Christ, I want to be more than I have ever been before, I want to do more than I have ever done before, and I want to reach out for more life than I have ever had before. And no-one, nothing in life does that for me the way Christ does.

That is the way it is because that is the way God has created it to be. Jesus has come into the world to be the Lord of all life, and the God we have come to know in him is the source of everything that is good in life. When we are in his company, we discover that we are not just enduring, but living; not just getting by, but having abundance. I have called him Lord for over sixty years now, and I have never, for even one moment, regretted the decision to commit my life to him. And, if you were to ask me where else you might have a chance of finding the good life, I haven't the foggiest idea of where else you might look. You can climb every mountain, ford every stream, follow every rainbow, but if that rainbow does not lead to Christ, you will miss it, and life will pass you by.

Let me remind you again that your dream, that on which you look for meaning in life will demand all you have to give. And something occupies that place of priority in your life right now. Something, right now, is ultimately real to you and ultimately important to you. You are depending upon something to make life good for you. And, whatever that something is, is your god, and everything else must take a back seat to it.

The number one sin in the Bible is idolatry. And, the number one sin of contemporary life is also idolatry. Idolatry is not worshipping a little statue; idolatry is placing anyone or anything in the place that belongs to God. When you do that, nothing in life works out very well, because life is designed to function in a God-centered way.

That is why God will not take a back seat to anyone or anything else. You can't place your job at the center of your dream and have God too. You can't put your family at the center of your dream and have God too. God insists upon first place in your loyalty. If you place anyone or anything in the place where He should be, it won't work. It just won't. But, listen now, when God is in the center of your life where He belongs, every other good thing is enhanced! God doesn't take life away from us, He gives it to us: rich, overflowing, abundant life. Do you hear the good news in that?

Why can't we trust that which is the clear central theme of scripture? So many people play games with it. They give something else first place in their lives and then tack on a little worship, a little prayer, a little Bible study there at the outside edges of their lives. What they are saying is that life, the abundant life, is really to be found somewhere else. And, it is in that somewhere else that they invest their deepest loyalty. Well, I'm here to tell you, it won't work! It never has and never will. Jesus said, "Seek *first* the Kingdom of God." First. First. Get that straight and everything else gets straight. But, if you try to put anything else first, it just won't work out very well.

Won't you give this the serious attention it deserves? If Jesus is who he says he is, then the God he makes known to us is the only One who deserves our highest loyalty. If Jesus is not who he says he is, then he is an impostor, a fraud, and he is not worthy of our attention. But, don't you see, the most irrational of all stances is to be half-hearted in our discipleship and to "sort of" follow Jesus. Maybe, just maybe Jesus knew what he was talking about when he said, "I am the way, I am the light". We already know a great many things that won't work. The only way to know for sure whether or not his way will work is for us to try it. Why not?

Let me wrap it up like this: a new pastor came to the church. He knocked on the door of some of the members one day. The husband was not there, but he visited for awhile with the wife. When the husband returned, she told him about the visit. "What did he say?" asked the husband. "It was the strangest thing," she said. He asked, "Does Christ live here?" "Well", the husband said, 'I hope you told him that we are respectable, God-fearing people." "He didn't ask that," she said. He asked, "Does Christ live here." "Surely you told him that we read the Bible and say our prayers," he said. "But, he didn't ask that," she said. "He asked, 'Does Christ live here?'" "We go to worship every Sunday. Surely you told him that," said the husband. "I told him all of that," she said, "but all he asked was, 'Does Christ live here?'"

The essential question, that. Listen, you can climb every mountain, you can ford every stream, you can follow every rainbow and search high and low for your dream. But, if Christ does not live where you live, then you are missing it. Listen to Jesus again, and remember that Jesus always keeps his promises: "I have come that you may have life, and have it abundantly. I am the light of the world. Whoever follows me will not walk in darkness, but will have the light of life." I trust that!

Prayer: God, our Father, we are searching because we need that which the rest of life cannot provide. You plant the dream in our hearts and You make us restless and dissatisfied until we pursue it, and find it, and finally come to rest in Your love and in Your will. Forgive us when we stubbornly insist upon pursuing our dream down all those dead end streets which promise so much and deliver so little. Come to us again in Jesus, claim us as Your own, and give us that life which is full, and satisfying, and abundant. In the name of Jesus, the light of the world, we pray. Amen.

My Favorite Things

Philippians 4:8-9

I have acknowledged that I am a pushover for happy endings. I like it when love wins out and when goodness prevails. Since this is the last chapter talking about the musical, "The Sound of Music." I want you to know it does have a happy ending. Maria and the captain get married and the children are delighted. The Nazis take over Austria and the captain was ordered to report for duty in the navy of the Third Reich, but instead the captain, Maria, and their seven children escaped from Austria and lived a full and happy life in the free world. Since the musical is based on historic events, I am happy to report that the captain and Maria had three additional children born to their marriage, making a total of ten! And, as all such musicals require, they all lived happily ever after.

But back to the earlier part of the story: shortly after Maria arrived at von Trapp manor to become governess, there was a terrible thunderstorm that shook the whole house. Gretl, the youngest of the children, came running into Maria's room in fear. Maria gathered her into her arms and asked, "Where are the others?" Gretl said, "They're asleep. They're not scared." About that time there was another earth rattling thunder clap, and the four other girls came running in for refuge and assurance. They all got into Maria's bed, and Maria said, "Now, all we have to do is wait for the boys." One of the girls said, "You won't see them. Boys are brave." There was another thunder clap and the two boys came running in. Maria said, "You boys weren't scared too, were you?" Friedrich, the older boy said, "O no! We just wanted to be sure that you weren't." "That's very thoughtful of you, Friedrich," Maria said. When another thunder clap shook the house, Gretl, the little one, asked, "Why does it do that?" Maria answered, "Well, the lightning says something to the thunder and the thunder answers back." Gretl continued, "Why does the thunder get so angry? It makes me want to cry." Maria said, "When something happens to me and I begin to be unhappy, I just try to think of nice things." "What kind of things?" the children asked. "Nice things," Maria said. "Let me see…" And she begins to sing. Let's listen…

"Raindrops on roses and whiskers on kittens,
Bright copper kettles and warm woolen mittens,
Brown paper packages tied up with strings,
These are a few of my favorite things.
Cream colored ponies and crisp apple strudels,
Doorbells and sleigh bells and schnitzel with noodles,
Wild geese that fly with the moon on their wings,
These are a few of my favorite things.
Girls in white dresses with blue satin sashes,
Snowflakes that stay on my nose and eyelashes,
Silver white winters that melt into springs,
These are a few of my favorite things.
When the dog bites, when the bee stings,
When I'm feeling sad,
I simply remember my favorite things,
And then I don't feel so bad."

That's not a bad philosophy, because the human mind cannot focus, really focus, on more than one thing at a time. Whatever it is you are focusing on pushes everything else out of your consciousness. When you are thinking about "raindrops on roses and whiskers on kittens", you cannot be thinking about thunder and lightning at the same time.

That is what Paul was getting at in the scripture from Philippians, "Whatever is true, whatever is honorable, whatever is just, whatever is pure, whatever is pleasing, whatever is commendable…think on these things." As long as you are thinking about such things that ennoble life, you cannot be thinking of those things that make life more base and dirty. And, as I have noted, a basic truth about life is that we tend to become like that with which we associate on a continual basis. Think about that. Since that is true, what makes sense to me is that we decide what kind of person we want to be, then we surround ourselves with the kinds of thoughts and experiences that will help us to become that person. That way we shape our becoming intentionally, rather than allowing our lives to be shaped in a haphazard way. That makes sense to me.

If you have positive experiences and positive thoughts, they tend to expel negative thoughts and fears. Somewhere I heard about a woman in Kansas City who went into a Haagen-Daz store one day to purchase an ice cream cone. After making her selection and paying for it, she turned to leave. Suddenly, she found herself looking into the big blue eyes of Paul Newman, who was in town filming a picture. He smiled at her and said, "Hello!" Seeing him there made her knees shake. She left the shop with her heart pounding in excitement. When she got to her car and regained her composure, she realized that she did not have her ice cream cone. She hurried back to the store to get it and met Paul Newman again at the door. "Are you looking for your ice cream cone?" he asked. She nodded, unable to speak. He smiled and said, "You put it in your purse with your change." Do you get the point? Once you get excited about Paul Newman, you forget about ice cream!

Too often we religious people attempt to overcome negative influences just by trying harder. We say to ourselves, "Don't do that. Don't think about that." Let's try that. Don't think about the color black. Try very hard not to think about the color black. Isn't it true that the harder we try, the more we think about the color black? By concentrating on it, we give it power.

But there is a better way. If you want to get rid of a negative, the way to do it is to overpower it with a stronger, positive influence. You don't want to think about the color black? Well then, think of the color red. Think about the beautiful red in a flaming sunset. Think about the luscious red of a fresh tomato sandwich. Think about the juicy red middle of a luscious watermelon. Think red! Isn't it true that while you were thinking red, you had forgotten black?

That is the way it works: think red, forget about black; think about Paul Newman, forget about ice dream; think about "brown paper packages tied up with string" and you forget about thunder and lightning. You think about what is true, what is honorable, what is just, and what is pure, and you can't think of things less noble at the same time.

Maria was trying to help the children overcome their fear. She gave them some positive, enjoyable things to think about and take their minds off their fear. That's good psychology. But we Christians have a better way. Instead of just thinking about "bright copper kettles and warm woolen mittens," we turn to what the church calls, "holy habits," or "the means of grace." Maria knew about them. And, when the going got tough, beyond the fear of thunder and lightning, that is what she turned to as well...holy habits, means of grace.

We who live by faith believe that God's grace is the one thing that will overcome everything that troubles us. So, as long as grace is at work in our lives, we can face anything; we can deal with anything. O, grace does not always remove the trouble, but it gives us what we need to deal with trouble. That's what we sing about in "Amazing Grace:" "Through many dangers, toils and snares I have already come; 'tis grace has brought me safe thus far, and grace will lead me home."

The Christian community has taught, and my experience confirms, that God is always ready to give us all the grace we need. In fact, God is more willing to give it to us than we are to receive it. So, the only thing necessary for us to do is to become receptive. Listen now, because I'm going to say something important: for two thousand years now, Christians have known that there are certain things we can do which will lower our barriers and make us accessible to God, so that He can give us the grace we need. There are certain things we can do to put us in those places where grace is most likely to take hold of us. So, rather than just thinking about our favorite things, we intentionally do those things which will cause grace to flow into our lives.

Let me give you an example: our family lived in Arizona for five years. The desert there is beautiful, but it can be treacherous if you don't understand it and respect it. Every year, I read in the newspapers about people who drowned in the desert. They would come out from the east, find a nice, smooth place in the desert to pitch their tent, not knowing that they were camping in a dry river bed. Then, it would rain in the mountains and a wall of water would come rushing down that river bed and people would drown. Now, here is the lesson drawn from that: if you are in the desert and you want to get wet, go to a dry river bed and stand there, because when water flows in the desert, that is where it will be. That is where water has always flowed in the desert.

In that same way, Christians have learned that there are certain places where grace flows. So, if you want to deal with the difficulties of life by immersing yourself in grace, just begin to use these "holy habits," these "means of grace." I want to suggest five of them.

Prayer is the first. Brother Lawrence called it "practicing the presence of God." When Maria first went to be the governess of the seven von Trapp children, she was nervous and apprehensive. On her journey she sang, "I have confidence in me!" But when she arrived at the gate to von Trapp manor, she wilted. And she prayed simply, "O help!" That's a pretty good prayer! I have come to believe that prayer, rightly understood, is anything you do with a conscious awareness of God. So, we turn our thoughts to God and open ourselves to His Spirit. We listen to what He has to say. We open our hands to receive what He has to give. We allow ourselves to be shaped and molded in His presence. And, in that way we receive His grace which provides guidance and comfort and strength.

The reading of scripture is the second. When we understand it, the Bible is the spiritual diary of two groups of people. The Old Testament is the spiritual diary of the people of Israel. The New Testament is the spiritual diary of the new Israel, or the church. As we read about these ancient encounters with God, that same God – Who is still alive and at work – that same God meets us there and speaks His word to us right here, right now. So, the Bible is not so much the word God *spoke* as it is the word God *speaks*.

I will never forget the moment I was told that I had cancer of the prostate. As soon as the doctor spoke that word, cancer, some words popped into my mind, words I had not thought about for over fifty years. No doubt they had been placed there by my mother because they are in King James English. The words are from Isaiah: "Thou shalt keep him in perfect peace whose mind is stayed on Thee." Those ancient words came to my mind and they stayed with me throughout my surgery and recovery. They were not just ancient words, they were the means by which I opened myself to God and He did, during that bout with sickness, exactly what the words described. I did not experience any apprehension throughout those difficult weeks. God does keep His promises!

Someone said that you open the Bible for the same reason you open a telephone book: you want to get in touch with someone. Of course, for us, that Someone is God. And, meditating upon scripture is a primary means of getting in touch with God and opening ourselves to His gift of grace.

Fasting is a third means of grace. It is true that withdrawal from food for a period of time would not hurt most of us a bit. But fasting is more than that. It is the taking on of a spiritual discipline, so that we can focus upon our relationship with God for a prolonged period of time. Going on a retreat is a similar spiritual discipline which accomplishes much the same thing as a fast.

Association with other persons of faith is the fourth means of grace. When Maria panicked over her loving feelings for the captain, instinctively she knew that she could receive help back at the abbey with the nuns, and especially with the mother abbess. When I think back over my life, it is clear that so many of God's blessings have been given to me through other people. Again and again God has blessed me with His grace, given through people. It has been suggested that when we are with loving friends, our joys are doubled and our sorrows are cut in half. That is the way it is because we were not created for isolation, but for community. We can face anything, we can deal with anything as long as we do not have to face it alone and loving friends are with us. I am not always strong and faithful. But, when I am weak, I can ride piggy-back on the faith of those who are strong. Then, when they are weak, they can ride piggy-back on my strength, and together we can make it!

Acts of love and compassion are a fourth means of grace. Whenever we reach out to others in loving ways we find ourselves receiving love as well. When we pass on to others the love we have received from God, the channels of grace are opened up and grace flows to us. However, when we try to hoard the blessings of God selfishly, the channels become clogged and we become unable to receive. If you want to take your mind off your problems, your temptations, and your fears, find some hurting person and, in love, do something to help that person. Do that and you will find yourself being strengthened and encouraged in the process.

The fifth and final "holy habit" or means of grace I will mention is worship, especially the sacraments. Something good happens to us in worship. Don't ever underestimate the positive influence of a lifetime of habitual worship. It means so much to be with the "body of Christ" in worship, knowing that I am not the only one who has decided to follow Jesus. I am not the only one who is seeking daily to be a faithful disciple. In worship I am part of a family of faith, and together, we are in the presence of God. We sing, we pray, we give, we hear again the gospel story, and we commit ourselves anew to be followers of Jesus. And, in all of that we send our roots into the soil of God's grace and we receive what we need to be faithful. Do you understand now what I mean by "means of grace" or "holy habits?"

And, the more we do these things, the more efficacious they become. I like the way one person put it: "God waits on His regular customers first!" That doesn't mean that God plays favorites, or that we have to jump through religious hoops in order to earn God's favor. No, it simply means that the more we make ourselves available to God, the more grace He is able to give us.

It is through these "holy habits" that we receive love, forgiveness, guidance and strength. As I think about it, what else do we need? It is better than positive thinking. It is better than simply thinking about "favorite things". Like standing in the desert waiting for water, we engage in these holy habits waiting for grace, and then by God's grace, we are equal to anything!

Prayer: Loving Father, we are grateful that You are more ready to give us Your gift of grace than we are to receive it. And, we thank You for giving us ways to make ourselves open to You, so that you can give us what we need. We are ready now to receive. Come to us and give us all that we need. We pray in the name of Jesus, Your gift of grace to us. Amen.

Good Night My Someone

Acts 17:22-28; John 1:18

During my junior high, high school, and college years I was a trumpet player, and band was an important part of my life. I would rather play my trumpet than eat, still would, and I love to eat! In fact, I almost became a band director. That was my vocational plan until God got involved and pointed me in a different direction. Music has always been an important part of my life. It is not surprising, then, that I have always loved Broadway musicals, and of those, "The Music Man" is one of my all-time favorites.

There are a great many catchy, "sing-able," whistleable tunes in the score, and I was tempted to choose a number of them for this book. I would delight in seeing some of the musicians I have known stage a rousing rendition of "Seventy-six Trombones." I would love to select members of the school board quartet to sing "Lida Rose," especially if I could sing one of the parts. I love good barber shop singing! And I would especially love seeing and hearing some people I know singing, "We've got trouble, right here in River City, and that's spelled with "T" which rhymes with "P" and that stands for pool!" The trouble with all those songs is that I could think of no way to attach meditations to them, and, after all, this is supposed to be about the connection between Broadway songs and the gospel, not simply a musical review. So, some songs are not appropriate.

One song, though, that has been tickling my imagination is "Good Night My Someone." I keep coming back to that one. Let me give you the story line. Professor Harold Hill is a traveling con artist, a very persuasive and even lovable con artist, but a con artist nonetheless. He goes from town to town selling band instruments and uniforms, promising to form a boys' band. Of course, he never stays anywhere long enough to form a band. There is a part of him that would like to, but he can't read even a note of music. So, he just pulls his con, collects the money, and moves on, one step ahead of the sheriff.

Then he comes to River City, Iowa. Just another town filled with gullible people, he thought. But what happened there changed his life forever. There in River City was an unmarried young woman named Marian. She was the local librarian and piano teacher who lived with her mother and her little brother, Winthrop. The mother is on a constant search for a husband for Marian. She feels that her daughter is being too "picky," and that time is running out. She says, "The stranger with the suitcase may be your very last chance." But Marian is not convinced.

One night Marian is giving a piano lesson to Amaryllis, a little girl who has a crush on Winthrop. But Winthrop is shy, and self conscious about his lisp, so he doesn't encourage Amaryllis at all. Marian and Ameryllis walk over to the open window and look up into the evening sky. Ameryllis is telling Marian about her feelings for Winthrop. She says, "I say 'good night' to him on the evening star every night, and he never says anything to me. If a girl doesn't have a sweetheart, who's she going to say 'good night' to on the evening star?" Marian replies, "Well, for the time being, you can just say, 'Good night my…my someone.' And then you can put the name in when the right someone comes along." "All right", says Amaryllis, "it's better than nothing." "Yes it is," says Marian, and she begins to sing:

> "Good night, my someone, good night my love,
> Sleep tight my someone, sleep tight my love;
> A star is shining its brightest light
> For good night, my love, for good night.
> Sweet dreams be yours, dear, if dreams there be,
> Sweet dreams to carry you close to me;
> I wish they may and I wish they might,

Now good night my someone, good night.
True love can be whispered from heart to heart
When lovers are parted, they say,
But I must depend on a wish and a star
As long as my heart doesn't know who you are."

Marian knew that there was someone out there who would love her, someone whom she would love in return. She knew it. She sensed it deep within her. But, she didn't know his name. And in the meanwhile, she wouldn't settle for just anyone. It had to be her "someone" special. Did you note those poignant words in her song, "I must depend on a wish and a star as long as my heart doesn't know who you are."

That is where my active imagination got hooked. Often I talk about our relationship with God and our relationship with others as connected with each other. So, it should not be surprising that I connected Marian's longing for her "someone" with our longing for God. When she began to sing, "Good night my someone," I immediately began to think of Paul's experience in Athens. There, in Athens, on Mars Hill, he was standing in the midst of pagan altars, scores of them. There was an altar to this god and that god and the other god. The Athenians were very religious people, as Paul noted. And there, amidst all the altars, there was one bearing the inscription, "To an unknown god." They sensed that there was "Someone" whose name they did not know. Paul seized the moment and said, "What you worship as unknown, this I proclaim to you." Then, he proceeded to preach the Christian gospel, saying that God is not far away, but very close to every one of us; indeed He is the One in whom we live and move and have our being. And, because of Jesus, we know who He is and what He is like. As the gospel of John puts it, "No one has ever seen God; but the only son who is close to the Father's heart, he has made Him known."

Do you see the connection, or am I the only one whose mind and heart are wired this way? There is Marian, the librarian, singing, "Good night my someone…I must depend upon a wish and a star as long as my heart doesn't know who you are." There is Marian, singing about this someone whose name she doesn't know, and there are the Athenians building an altar to a God whose name and nature they do not know. But both are sensing deep within themselves that there is someone there. Listen now: the God who has created us, and placed within us a

longing for a special someone to love and marry and share life with us –
that same God has placed another longing within us, a longing for Him!

We all know that feeling, don't we? The God who has created the
world and everything in it, created you and me to live in a loving, trusting
relationship with Him. And, we sense in our depths that life will never
be what it is supposed to be until we are in that relationship. We may
not understand that fully. We may not have the words to express it. But,
within every one of us there is that wistful longing, not unlike that of
Marian longing for her someone, longing for a relationship with God.

It expresses itself in a variety of ways. There is loneliness, knowing
that there is Someone with whom we should be connected. There is
homesickness, knowing that, apart from God, we are not centered where
we belong. There is restlessness, moving from here to there, from this
to that, searching for something...something. There is anxiety: often
anxiety is not a sign of God's absence, but a sign of God's presence,
calling to us, nudging us to relationship with Himself. We can express
it in a variety of ways, but it all comes down to the fact that at the center
of life there is a God shaped empty place. We can spend our days trying
to fill the void with this or that. But nothing else will satisfy, because the
empty place is God shaped. Augustine was right on target when he said,
"Thou hast made us for Thyself, O God, and our hearts are restless 'til
they find their rest in Thee."

Most of the people I know spend their every day in this restless,
anxious search for something which will fill the void. They search
through their jobs, through their hobbies, through their pleasures. They
are searching, but they don't know what they are searching for. It is just
as Marian sang, "My heart doesn't know who you are." But something
important is missing, everyone knows that. Even the non-religious
folks who never show up for worship, who would never use religious
language, still know. Someone is calling to them. Someone is pulling
at their hearts. It's true, isn't it? We all sense that there is Someone -
Someone who will put all the pieces together and finally make life what
it is supposed to be.

The Athenians sensed that, beyond their pantheon of gods, there was
Someone they had missed. So, Paul proceeded to tell them and us who
He is. I like the way the gospel of John expressed it: "No one has ever seen
God; but the only son who is close to the Father's heart, he has made Him
known." Who is this Someone our hearts tell us is there, this Someone

who calls to us in our depths, this Someone who tugs at our coat sleeves, and makes us restless 'til we find our rest in Him? The scriptures say that He is God, and He has been made known to us in Jesus.

I don't have a vocabulary large enough to tell you what good news that is, that this Someone we sense in our depths is like Jesus. I will say more about that in a later chapter, but for now let me add this: just imagine that this Someone of whom we have been vaguely aware has a friendly face and His name is love! That is incredibly good news!

You see, primitive people had a different picture of god, or the gods. For them, god was someone to fear. And most of the practices of their religion were attempts to appease the anger of god, to keep god from hurting them or doing bad things to them. The idea was just to get god off their backs – appeasement. Their god was reluctant to do good things for them. So, their religion was an attempt to manipulate god. They wanted to do all they could to persuade god to give them large families, good crops, healthy bodies, and prosperous lives. They believed that they had to manipulate god into giving them all that because, basically, god was reluctant to do anything good for them. Do you get the picture? Appeasement. Manipulation. (I said that was primitive religion, but it sounds a great deal like much of what passes for Christianity in our time!) Don't buy it. That is not the gospel!

Listen! The good news is that the God made known to us in Jesus is not against us. He is for us. He doesn't have to be appeased or manipulated. We don't have to beg or bargain with Him. Our God wants to give good things to us even more than we want to receive them. God wants to love us, forgive us, bless us, claim us as His children, and give us that life which Jesus called "abundant." You can understand, then, why the Christian story is called "good news". That is what the word "gospel" means. When we finally came to understand that God is like Jesus, then for the first time we could be glad about God!

Do you get the picture? That Someone we sense in our depths is not remote, uncaring, threatening. No, Jesus said that He is like a father, and He loves us more than we will ever fully understand. The good news is that there is nothing we can do to make God stop loving us. Further, there is nothing we can do to make God love us more than He already does. Life becomes good for us when we fill in the blanks and finally come to understand that the Someone we meet in the deep places of life is like Jesus.

So, you don't have to search any longer. You don't have to speculate any longer. As Marian said to Amaryllis, "You can put the name in when the right someone comes along." Well, according to Jesus, the name of that Someone is God. And He is like a father!

To close this chapter, I want to tell you about a friend of mine, a former pastor, with whom I was in seminary. He was always a good student, with a quick and brilliant mind. I haven't seen him in a while now, but I'll never forget the last time we were together. Through the years he had poured over the writings of philosophers and theologians. He had looked at all the coarse, ragged edges of life, and he had concluded that there is no God. He told me about his lost faith, and he said to me, "Jim, I don't have anyone to love me. I don't have anyone to forgive me. I don't have anyone to affirm me. I have to do all of that for myself." But even as he spoke, his eyes welled up with tears, in longing for the very God his words denied.

Jesus would say to him, "No, you're wrong. There is Someone to love you. There is Someone to forgive you. There is Someone to affirm you. There is!" Jesus made Him known. And Jesus called Him, "our Father."

Prayer: Our Father, we are grateful that we can call you our Father. We are grateful that the One we meet in our depths is like Jesus and that when we get to know You, we know that You have the face of love. Help us to know that. Help us to trust that. And help us to live our lives in the joy and security of that. We pray in the name of Jesus who made You known. Amen.

'Til There Was You

John 10:10

"The Music Man" is about a traveling con man, Professor Harold Hill, who goes from town to town selling band instruments and uniforms promising to form a boys' band. But he never does it, however much he would like to, because he can't read music, and because he has never led a band. So, he just makes his fraudulent sales, pockets the money, and leaves town just a step ahead of the sheriff.

He arrives in the little town of River City, Iowa, to run his con again. From the beginning almost everyone in town was caught up in his mesmerizing talk of a boys' band. Almost everyone that is, except Marian, the local librarian and piano teacher. She does some research and discovers that his credentials are phony, confirming what she has suspected all along. But, over several days, in spite of her better judgment, she begins to fall in love with this lovable con man.

She is moved by what she sees happening to her little brother, Winthrop, and to all the other people in this dull, sleepy little town, as they are caught up in the music man's dream of a boy's band. Her little brother is a sad, shy, and introverted little boy. Their father had died just two years earlier, and Winthrop had taken it very hard. But, when he listened to the music man talk, and especially when he got his very own shiny, brass cornet, it changed his life. He smiled. He talked with a twinkle in his eye. He walked with a livelier step. So, Marian threw away the damning evidence she had found against the professor and decided to love him anyway!

Toward the end of the musical, the town had found out how they had been defrauded, and a mob set out to hunt him down. Of course, Winthrop was shattered! The one he had believed in so much had let him down. In tears, he went running home, only to find the professor and his sister there, talking.

Winthrop said to him, "I wish you had never come to River City!" Marian said, "No you don't Winthrop." "Sister, do you believe him?" he asked. "I believe everything he ever said." "But he promised us..." "I know what he promised, and it all happened just like he said: the lights, the colors, the cymbals and the flags." Winthrop asked, "What was all of that?" Marian replied, "In the way every kid in this town walked around all summer, and looked and acted – especially you – and the parents too."

Marian described what she had experienced and what the whole town had experienced when the music man came to town by singing this song...

> "There were bells on the hill, but I never heard them ringing,
> No, I never heard them at all, 'til there was you.
> There were birds in the sky, but I never saw them winging,
> No, I never saw them at all, 'til there was you.
> And there was music, and there were beautiful roses, they tell me,
> In sweet, fragrant meadows of dawn and dew;
> There was love all around, but I never heard it singing,
> No, I never heard it at all, 'til there was you."

What a marvelous song! I have to tell you that the musical had a happy ending. The townspeople captured the professor and were about to do what mobs do. In the meanwhile, the children had put on their uniforms, gotten their instruments, and gathered at the city hall. The people decided to give him one last chance to prove himself. And there, with the kind of miracle reserved only for Broadway musicals, the children began to play the "Minuet in G", using the professor's improbable "think system". Of course, the music was awful. But the tune was recognizable. And the parents, looking and listening with the eyes and ears of love, were so overwhelmed by the performance of their children that they let the professor off the hook. And, we assume, he and Marian got married and lived happily ever after! That's the story of "The Music Man."

But you know me well enough by now to know that my mind and heart are strangely wired. And, every time I hear that song about the difference Harold Hill made by coming to River City, Iowa, I can't help thinking about the difference Jesus has made by coming into the world, and into my life and yours.

Some friends once gave me a plaque that read, "Life is now in session. Are you present?" The longer I live the more I realize how easy it is to be absent from life. You know what I am talking about: looking without seeing, listening without hearing, chewing without tasting, and existing without living. God has made a good world and placed us in it, intending for life to be good for us. Really *good*. But so many people live their lives in a one dimensional, dull gray world, allowing the fullness of life to pass them by. As that good theologian Auntie Mame put it: "Life is a banquet, and most poor suckers are starving to death!"

No-one wants that. Everyone wants to live fully, meaningfully, and enjoyably. We don't want any good thing to pass us by. I remember hearing about a little boy whose father was in the army and stationed far from home. He knew that his father's work was dangerous and that there was a chance that he could be killed. So, he wrote a letter to express his love and concern. He didn't express it exactly as he intended, but I like what he said. He wrote, "Dear daddy, I hope you will be alive as long as you live!" That's what we all want, isn't it? We want to be alive as long as we live!

Clearly, that is what God wants for us. That is why He sent Jesus to us. As Jesus said, "I have come that you may have life, and have it abundantly!" That is why the gospel is such good news: the very thing we all want so much is exactly what Jesus has come to give us: LIFE!

How does he do that? He starts by helping us get the relationships of life straightened out, with God at the center. In the presence of Jesus, we meet a God who is not against us, but for us. We meet a God who wants to give us every good thing in life, a God who is like a loving father, in the best sense of that word. That God is to be at the center of life, giving meaning and direction to everything else. The God we come to know in Jesus does not want us to go through life bearing burdens too heavy for us to bear, so He offers to take them away. He wants to lighten our load, not add to it. He does that by taking away the guilt of our sin through the marvelous gift of forgiveness. And, He takes away all the regrets of the past, helping us to stop the useless saying, "If only... If only I had not done that...If only I had not said that...If only I had taken advantage of that opportunity..." He cuts us free from all of that and gives us a new future, open with new possibilities and assuring us that He is in the business of creating new futures. I tell you, there is hope in that. There is new life in that.

And, once we allow that loving, forgiving, gracious relationship with God to change us, He begins to make that spill over into all the other relationships of life. Because we are loved, we are able to love. Because we are forgiven, we are able to forgive. God helps us to grow into people less obsessed with getting and more concerned with giving. He enlarges the circle of our concern to include the whole world, and sets us to the task of reaching out in love. We begin to really care about others.

The God we come to know in Jesus shows us how life can best be lived and savored for ourselves and shared with others. He opens our eyes, ears, and hearts to all the wonders of the world which are placed here as expressions of His extravagant love for us. He invites us to live and love and enjoy life in the warmth and security of His love! The best way to say it is that when we are in company of Jesus, our experience of life is not narrowed, but enlarged. We come alive to all of life!

While writing this, I remembered the very first sermon I ever preached. I was a nineteen year old college student and I was appointed pastor of a small, eighty-two member country church. The title of that sermon was "Following the Real Jesus." In truth, it was not much of a sermon. But the title was good and the idea behind it was sound, because if we are to be followers of Jesus, it had better be the real Jesus. There are too many counterfeits and imitations around!

There are people who talk a great deal about Jesus, but the Jesus they describe is not one I know. And, I have to say, he is not one I want to know. Many people who talk about Jesus sound more like Jesus' first century opponents than like Jesus himself. It is instructive to know that the people in the first century who opposed Jesus most vigorously and who succeeded in having him put to death were religious leaders. Religion is a powerful thing, and unfortunately its power can be used in destructive ways just as surely as in life enhancing ways. Read through the gospels and you will discover that the first century religious leaders thought that Jesus was not holy enough and not righteous enough.

Let me cite two areas in which Jesus was criticized. First, Jesus was not properly selective about the people with whom he associated, they said. The way they understood religion, righteous people were not supposed to associate with gentiles, Samaritans, and all the sorts of sinners in their midst. However, Jesus insisted that all were children of God, and even if they were not behaving their best, they still were of infinite worth and deserving of love for that very reason. So, Jesus associated with everyone and loved everyone. The religious leaders pointed accusing fingers and sneered, "Look at him! Look at him! He associates with sinners, and even eats with them."

I'm glad that Jesus is not too selective about his company. That means he will keep company with me and with you. He will take us just as we are, and then love us into new life. That's the real Jesus!

There was a second area of criticism: Jesus didn't keep all their rules, and they had a lot of rules. Their distorted religion said, "Do this. Don't do that. Don't do the other." There was a rule about how many steps you could take on the Sabbath; rules about what you could or could not eat; rules about what you must give to the Temple; rules about the sacrifices you must make for every different situation; even rules about who you could associate with. It had degenerated largely into a religion of rules.

Remember the time a little girl was brought to Jesus? She was sick. It was the Sabbath, but Jesus had compassion and healed the girl. The religious authorities said, "Look! He broke a rule!" Jesus just cut to the bottom line and said simply, "Is it better to do good or to do evil on the Sabbath?" In other words, Jesus said, you are missing the point. You strain at gnats and swallow camels. It's not about rules. It is simply about seeking to do what is pleasing to God. Simply that. Do you know why? Because what is pleasing to God is also what is best for us. What is pleasing to God opens life up for us and makes all of life abundant! That is the real Jesus!

Won't we finally understand? God is not the great patrolman in the sky seeking to cut down our speed. God is not a Grinch trying to take all the enjoyment out of life. God is not a taskmaster trying to make us jump through unnecessary religious hoops, add to our load, and make life more difficult for us. No, just the opposite. God wants us to experience all the best that life affords. He did not send Jesus into the world to take life away from us. Any version of Christianity that reduces the size of your world, that constricts your circle of love and concern, and that adds to your load rather than lightening it…any version of Christianity that turns your joy into sadness and your song into a dirge does not keep company with the real Jesus. Listen to the real Jesus: "I have spoken my words to you so that my joy may be in you, and so that your joy may be full. I have come that you may have life and have it abundantly!"

That has been my experience. When the God made known in Jesus became real to me and I made the response of faith, I couldn't help smiling. I felt cleaner than I had ever felt before. I felt free of guilt, free of anxiety, and free of the burden of life. There was a song in my heart and a new outlook on life. Clearly, I was a new person. Others have experienced it too. That is why they have talked of Jesus as bread for the hungry, water for the thirsty, light for those in darkness, and new life for those in "deadness."

I've been telling this story now for well over fifty years and I still can't get over it. I've seen it happen so many times: Some people are trying to earn their place in the world, trying to prove their worth by their performance, and are caught up in all the rules because they suspect that God really doesn't want us to enjoy life. Some are bogged down in guilt and can't believe that God loves and forgives us. Some are regular church goers who think they have experienced it all, but they have never been touched by God's grace. People in all these conditions suddenly come face to face with the Jesus of the gospels, God touches them with His amazing grace, and something happens! Something life changing happens! They see things they have never seen before. They feel things they have never felt before. They become more than they have ever been before. And they say something like, "I've never experienced anything like this before." The only way they know how to describe it is to say, "I was blind, but now I see. I was dead, but now I am alive, alive to all of life!"

I wonder how Marian's song would sound if we heard the words while thinking about Jesus? Read the words again, assuming they are describing our experience with Jesus:

"There were bells on the hill, but I never heard them
ringing,
No, I never heard them at all, 'til there was you.
There were birds in the sky, but I never saw them
winging,
No, I never saw them at all, 'til there was you.
And there was music, and there were beautiful roses,
they tell me,
In sweet, fragrant meadows of dawn and dew;
There was love all around, but I never heard it singing,
No, I never heard it at all, 'til there was you."

That is the real Jesus, and life is what he is about. Jesus said, "I have
come that you may have life, and have it abundantly."

Prayer: Father, forgive us when we are content to settle for counterfeit
and second best. Help us to know that You are a loving Father who wants
us to have the best that life affords. Cut us free now from all that inhibits
us and keeps us from fullness of life. Reach out to us through Your son,
Jesus, and give us that life which is life indeed. In his name we pray.
Amen.

A Cockeyed Optimist

Psalms 42:1-6

As you know by now, I love Broadway musicals. I am a pushover for musicals with hummable, whistleable tunes, an optimistic outlook, and a happy ending. After experiencing such a musical, I leave the theater with a smile on my face, with my pulse racing and my spirit soaring.

"South Pacific" did that for me. It opened on Broadway in April of 1949, shortly after the end of World War II. It ran for more than five years and won a Pulitzer Prize for drama in 1950, before being made into a motion picture in 1958. I loved it back then, and I love it now. Rogers and Hammerstein packed it with the kind of drama and music that has stayed with me. Of course, we couldn't include all the songs in this series. So, I decided early on not to feature "I'm Gonna Wash That Man Right Out of My Hair" or "There Is Nothing Like a Dame." But the songs we will talk about will do just fine!

The setting is an island in the South Pacific in the early years of World War II. Among the residents there, in addition to the military personnel, is a wealthy French planter, named Emile deBecque. Early in the musical, he is attracted to Ensign Nellie Forbush, a nurse attached to the base hospital, and the attraction is mutual. They come from very different worlds: he is an older, sophisticated Frenchman, she, a self-described "hick from the sticks of Little Rock, Arkansas." But, as they

 Hope

say in one of their songs, love has reasons that even wise men do not attempt to explain.

One day, Emile and Nellie are together in one of the gardens of his plantation. She shows him a clipping from her hometown newspaper, sent to her by her mother. There is a picture of her, and an article describing her as "Arkansas' own Florence Nightingale." Laughing, she said, "That picture was taken before I knew what rain and heat and mud can do to your disposition, but it isn't raining today!" Looking out at the horizon, she gushes, "Gosh, it's beautiful here! Just look at that yellow sun! And way out in the distance there, those lovely little white flowers!" Emile said, "Those little white flowers could easily be gunfire."

"How awful!" she said. "On such a day! Boys getting killed. People dead....But, you know, Emile, I don't think it's the end of the world as everyone else thinks. Do you?" "It's the end of some worlds," he said. "O, but not this one," she replies. "It can't be. I can't work myself up to getting that low. Do you think I'm crazy too? Well, they all do over at the base hospital. Do you know what they call me? 'Knucklehead Nellie.' I suppose I am, but I can't help it." And she begins to sing...

> "I'm stuck like a dope with a thing called hope, and I
> can't get it out of my heart."

What do you think? Is that naïve? Or is that reality at its deepest level?

For most of human history people were not very hopeful, and they did not want to be. They thought that hope was foolish. No, worse than that: they thought that hope was dangerous. The thinking was: if you have high hopes, you will just be disappointed. So, to save yourself that pain, just don't expect too much. Avoid hope.

I don't buy it. I believe that hope is essential to the good life. What breath is to the physical body, hope is to the human spirit. You can never live the best if you expect the worst. I don't know of anything more encouraging, more strengthening, or more life giving than hope.

John Claypool has written about an experiment conducted by the Department of Psychology in a well known university. The researchers wanted to identify the factors necessary for coping. They filled two vats equally full of water, and placed a rat of comparable age and size in each one. Of course, the little creatures instinctively began to swim. The only difference between the two vats was that the top of one was sealed shut, while the other was left open. The rat in the sealed vat quickly sensed a diminishing supply of oxygen, saw no way of escape, gave up, stopped swimming, sank to the bottom and drowned in less than four minutes. In contrast, the other rat, seeing the opening at the top and having unlimited amounts of oxygen available, swam for an incredible 36 straight hours until, mercifully, the experiment was stopped. The difference was hope, even in rats. If you expect the worst, you cannot live the best. You just can't. All my life I have heard: "As long as there's life, there's hope." The deeper truth is that "as long as there's hope, there is life." Even rats know that!

Something good happens to us when we have a positive outlook on life. We are happier and we live life at a higher quality when we look for and expect good things. I identify with the little boy who went with his parents to the local pet store to buy a puppy for his birthday. After looking at all the puppies available, the father said, "Have you found one you like?" The little fellow, pointing to a puppy furiously wagging his tail, said, "I like the one with the happy ending!" We all do. When we expect the best, we also live the best. We just do.

But there is something to the ancient fears as well. It's important to expect the best. It's essential to be hopeful about the future. But it must not be a false hope. It must not be just hoping in hope. That kind of shallow hope will not sustain us in a world at war, when terrorism is spreading, when we are threatened by cancer and aids and heart disease, when the budget deficit is spiraling out of control and the gap between rich and poor is widening, when people everywhere seem caught up in materialism and consumerism and the life of the spirit is given short shrift. In that kind of world it's not enough to say, "All will be well," "Hope for the best," "Look on the bright side," "Every day in every way things are getting better and better." No, such platitudes are mostly sentiment, and sentiment is not enough to sustain us when the going gets tough. The fact is that every day things do not get better and better. And such a shallow outlook *can* set us up for disappointment.

Nellie's hopeful outlook comes close to such shallow sentiment because she gives us no *reason* for her hope. Before we can have a sustainable hope, a hope that will not disappoint us, a hope that keeps on

Sustainable Hope / God

keeping on no matter what, that hope must be grounded in something solid and something utterly dependable.

For people of faith, the source of our hope is God. The scriptures declare and our experience confirms that, above all else, God is the One who is utterly steadfast and dependable. As I have often said: God is not one kind of God today and another kind of God tomorrow. He does not provide for us today and neglect us tomorrow. He does not love us today and reject us tomorrow. No, from everlasting to everlasting, God is God. At every moment He is at work for our good. He is loving enough to want to do us good and He is powerful enough to put some clout behind His caring. You can put your hope in that. As the Psalmist wrote: "Hope in God!"

In fact, a good case can be made for the assertion that it is the Judeo-Christian faith that has given the gift of hope to the world! Walter Brueggemann, a highly respected Old Testament scholar has made the bold assertion that prior to Judaism there was no sense of hope in the world. People did not look into the future and expect something good that they could not yet see. They especially did not look into the future and expect something better than the present. That came as a result of the faith of ancient Israel. They had hope even when the historical data argued against it. It was and it is remarkable.

When the Babylonians overran Israel and took the best and the brightest of the Jews into exile, it was the darkest time in Jewish history. Jewish people were taken away from their homeland, from the temple, from all their sources of meaning. They were placed in a foreign land, surrounded by strange people, an alien culture, idolatrous religion. What did they have to look forward to? What did they have to be hopeful about?

And yet…And yet! I think that's one of the great expressions of the Bible: and yet -nevertheless. No matter what is happening, or seems to be happening, there is still a reason for hope, because there is God!

There in a foreign land, in exile, the people continued to have hope. And, as Brueggemann put it, it was hope against the data. All of the data said, "Give up. No future. No good expectations. No way!" And yet, stubbornly, the Jewish people insisted upon hope. Their prophets talked about the future, about the coming of a great day, when "the earth will be filled with the knowledge of the glory of the Lord, as the waters cover the sea." Hope!

And, they were right. The day came when the people of Israel were able to return to their land, to Jerusalem, and to the temple. But, in the meanwhile, while they were still out there in that foreign land, instead of giving up and drowning like the hopeless rat, they were sustained by their hope. God was able to do some of the best things in the entire history of Judaism, because they continued to trust in Him. Listen now: the synagogue was born there in exile. If they could not worship in the Temple, at least they could gather together and study the scriptures. So, the synagogue came into being. And, because the study of the scriptures was important, they collected all of their sacred writings, and they created the Old Testament substantially as we know it today. Isn't that remarkable? That all happened there in the exile! They did some of the best things in the worst times, because they refused to give up. They had hope in God!

I like what one Rabbi said: "To the Jew there is only one unforgivable sin, and that is the sin of despair." Of course! As long as there is hope there is life. So, keep swimming. Keep swimming. There is hope, because there is God!

Of course, Christianity has continued to affirm and enlarge upon that idea. The Christian faith has a hopeful view of God, a hopeful view of humanity, a hopeful view of history. We believe that history is not wandering aimlessly. God allows it to take detours because He has given us freedom, but God is at work in history, and therefore it is moving toward a goal. That goal is the Kingdom of God. That's what Jesus was all about. The central theme of his preaching was the Kingdom of God, which means the centrality of God in the world and in our lives. It means putting God first, and allowing God to define and to give meaning and direction to everything else in life. And, in the crucifixion and resurrection of Jesus, we see that all we affirm about God is not just pretty rhetoric, it is real and it is powerful. In those events we see the strong hands of God twist the crown of thorns into a crown of glory. He's doing it still. All of us who have faith, trust that in such hands our lives are secure. That's what we read in I Peter: "We have been born anew to a living hope through the resurrection of Jesus Christ from the dead." In other words, our hope is not pie in the sky optimism. Our hope is based upon something that has happened. It is based upon things God has done in history. We look to the future with hope because of what we know God has done in the past.

And just look at what Christian hope has done. In the first century world, Christians were a tiny minority, and not a very promising minority at that. Paul said it when he wrote of those first century Christians: "Not many of you were wise by human standards, not many were powerful, not many of noble birth." There they were, a handful of nobodies, telling the story of a carpenter from Nazareth who had been put to death by the Romans, but who had risen from the dead. What kind of chance did they have in that Roman world, dominated by Roman power, Roman culture, and Roman wealth. And yet… There is that term again: and yet…

Wholly against the data, that little rag tag bunch with their story of Jesus toppled that Roman empire, and the Christian faith has spread throughout the world like wildfire. Wow! Don't ever look at the future and leave God out of that picture. It's never a clear picture until God is in it. The last word is never spoken until it is God's word. Because God is, because God is who God is, we can hope!

Do you know the name, Carlyle Marney? Carlyle Marney was a Baptist preacher who set the standard for a generation of preachers. He was a pulpit giant. But late in his life, he fell into a deep depression, and no matter what he did, he could not climb out of it. He was an avid gardener. One afternoon, while he was experiencing a dark time, a time of terrible emotional heaviness, he was sitting listlessly among his plants when a thought suddenly came to him: "Roses grow out of horse manure!" He was startled as the realization dawned on him that if the loveliest and the most fragrant of blossoms could emerge from the smelliest and most repulsive of substances, who was he to set limits on what the creator of this mysterious world could yet do!"

Do you believe in God? Do you believe that God is like Jesus? Do you believe that God is not only loving, but also powerful, and that He is at work in every moment for our good? Do you believe that finally, God and all that is of God will win? Well, I believe that. I really believe that. If you believe that too, then you can have hope. That hope will sustain you. And that sustaining hope will produce in you the very best quality of life.

So, thank you Rogers and Hammerstein for writing South Pacific and for helping us to reclaim our hope. As Hammerstein said once in an interview: "I just couldn't write anything without hope in it." I'm glad he couldn't, because we need that. God, we need that! So, sing on,

Nurse Nellie Forbush, and I'll sing along with you. I, too, am "stuck like a dope with a thing called hope" and I don't want it out of my heart. But I have a reason for my hope. And that reason is God!

Prayer: God, our Father, we place our trust in You. We trust who You are. We trust Who You have revealed Yourself to be in Jesus. And that trust shapes the way we look at the future. So, bring joy out of our sorrow. Bring life out of our death. And bring hope out of our despair. Through Jesus, in whose name we pray. Amen.

Happy Talk

Philippians 3:13-14

In the previous chapter, we met Emile deBecque, the French planter living on an island in the South Pacific, where there was a large American military base. He fell in love with Nurse Nellie Forbush, the unsophisticated girl from Little Rock, Arkansas, and the feeling was mutual. We began that chapter with a positive flair as Nellie sang "I'm just a cockeyed optimist!" saying "I'm stuck like a dope with a thing called hope and I can't get it out of my heart." In this chapter we meet some new characters in South Pacific. Lieutenant Joe Cable is a marine officer from Philadelphia, Pennsylvania, sent to the island with specific orders. He was to recruit a civilian, Emile deBecque, for a mission. deBecque was a planter who had lived in that area for a long time and knew it well. Together they were to climb to a vantage point high on Marie Louise Island to track the movement of Japanese ships, and to radio the information back to the base. It was an extremely dangerous assignment.

There on the island was a local, Tonkanese entrepreneur, called "Bloody Mary." She sold trinkets, grass skirts, boar's tooth bracelets, and shrunken heads to the sailors stationed there. She was quite a colorful character! And, she had a beautiful daughter, Liat. Of course, like all mothers, she wanted the best for her daughter. As soon as she saw Lieutenant Cable, she knew that he was the man for Liat. She wanted

Joe for her son-in-law. So, she put Joe Cable and Liat together, and, predictably, they fell in love, head-over-heel, mind numbingly, hopelessly in love! They spent as much time together as possible. It was romantic, it was exciting, and it was wonderful! One day they were out swimming, diving and kissing and holding hands and swimming. And they pulled up at the water's edge where Mary was sitting.

Smiling, she said, "You happy, Lieutellan? Jacques Berrea want to marry Liat. He ask again last night." Joe said, "You mean that old French planter you told me about? The one you despise? You can't let her marry a man like that." "He's white man too, and very rich." "I don't care," Joe said. "You can't let her marry him!" "Okay" she said, "Then you marry her. Lieutellan, you have good life here. I am rich. Since war I make two thousand dollar. War go on I make maybe more. Give all the money to you and Liat. You don't have to work. I work for you. All day long you and Liat play together, make love, talk happy." And she begins to sing about it…

> "Happy talk, keep talkin' happy talk. Talk about things
> you'd like to do.
> You got to have a dream, if you don't have a dream,
> How you gonna have a dream come true?
> Talk about the boy sayin' to the girl, 'Golly baby, I'm a
> lucky cuss'.
> Talk about the girl sayin' to the boy, 'You an' me is
> lucky to be us!'
> Happy talk, keep talkin' happy talk. Talk about things
> you'd like to do.
> You got to have a dream, if you don't have a dream,
> How you gonna have a dream come true?"

All my adult life, those words have stayed with me, bouncing around in my head and in my heart, and those are the words I want to focus on in this chapter: "You've got to have a dream. If you don't have a dream, how're you going to have a dream come true?"

It was Mary's dream that Joe and Liat marry and live happily together on the island. Mary saw herself with them and her future grandchildren in a wonderful life. That was her dream. What is yours? What is mine?

It's clear to me that almost all of the good things that happen in life start with a dream. Someone dreams a dream, catches a vision of what can be, and then they begin working to make the dream come true. It's the dream that excites us, inspires us, and motivates us. Without a dream we just plod aimlessly through our every day, going nowhere in particular, having no goal greater than getting through the day. From my high school days, I remember someone describing that kind of life like this:

> "Where are you going with that shovel? To dig a ditch.
> Why? To earn money. Why? To buy food. Why? To keep
> strong. Why? So I can dig ditches."

Such is the life without a dream. You go through the motions of living, but there is no meaning and no purpose any greater than survival. I remember hearing years ago about the little town of Flagstaff, Maine. It was to be taken over as a part of a hydroelectric development. The town was to be vacated, then submerged beneath water as a huge dam was to be built to generate electric power. An interesting thing happened: in the months before people moved out, all repairs and improvements to homes and other buildings came to a dead stop. After all, what's the point of painting a house if it is going to be covered with water in six months? Why fix anything? So, week by week, the little town became more and more run down and shabby. It became a slum area long before it was submerged. It's true, isn't it? When there is no dream of the future, there is no motivation for today.

You've got to have a dream. And, I tell you, there is power there if it's the right dream. Throughout history, the greatest things have been done by people who were motivated by great dreams. Christopher Columbus dreamed of reaching the east by sailing west. He risked himself for his dream, discovered America, and connected Europe with this great continent. The founders of this country dreamed of a nation with liberty and justice for all. They invested their lives in the pursuit of their dream, and here we are today. The Wright brothers dreamed of flight, and on that day at Kitty Hawk, they made their dream come true. The people who came after them dreamed of space exploration, of putting a man on the moon and even on Mars. Martin Luther King had a dream of a world where all people could sit down together at the table of brotherhood. You get the point: time and time again, great things have been accomplished by people who were motivated by a great dream.

I like what the artist, Raphael, once said in describing his art work. He said, "I dream dreams and I see visions. Then I simply paint around my dreams and visions." That's the way it has been with people of greatness. The dream has come first, then the reality.

Bloody Mary had a dream that was pretty good. She understood that happiness and fulfillment in life has more to do with relationships than anything else. Life can be pretty good if we are loved and if we love. Of course, it would have been nice if her dream had also embraced a larger world, and if it had made room for God. But her dream was far better than most.

That reminds us that not just any dream will do. You've got to have a dream, but it's got to be the right kind of dream. There are far too many people who get caught up in the wrong dreams. And, I suppose the thing I fear more than anything else is that so much in our culture encourages us to pursue the wrong values, to get excited about the wrong things, to set the wrong priorities, and to dream the wrong dreams. We are like the passengers on an airplane one day who were addressed by the pilot. He said over the intercom: "Attention. This is the Captain speaking. I have bad news and good news. First, the bad news: our radar has gone out, we are hopelessly lost, we are losing altitude fast, and we are almost out of fuel. Now the good news: we're making awfully good time!"

That's what I fear: that we are encouraged to go full speed in the wrong direction. So much in our culture tells us: "Look out for yourself first. Be successful whatever it takes. Make money and have fun!" I don't know how you hear that, but to me, it has a hollow ring to it. Those goals are not big enough to satisfy us. Those dreams are a great many sizes too small.

Let me tell you where the best dreams start. The best dreams always start with God. We then take hold of His vision and we begin to dream God's dream after Him. I think that's where all the best dreams start.

That's where it started with the Apostle Paul. When we first meet him in the New Testament, Paul is nodding his approval as the Christian, Stephen, is stoned to death. Then, he too, begins to persecute the Christians. But then he had a conversion experience, and from the time he had his conversion experience on the road to Damascus, to the end of his life, he was energized and motivated by a great dream. His life was not fragmented. He did not dissipate his energies by going off in a dozen different directions. No, he pursued his dream with a single-minded devotion. He allowed nothing to interfere with it. Listen to him: "This one thing I do: forgetting what lies behind and straining forward to what lies ahead, I press on toward the goal for the prize of the heavenly call of God in Christ Jesus."

Paul had a God-given dream, and he was never satisfied until that dream became a reality. No matter how much he accomplished, he never felt that he had done enough. The conversion of the entire world? "Why not?" says Paul. "I have a dream! This one thing I do!"

It's true: the best dreams always start with God. My father was fond of saying, "When God created you, He dreamed a beautiful dream of the person you would become." And God built into you all the attributes and inclinations to enable you to become that person. Don't ever forget that you are a unique and unrepeatable miracle of God's creative power. No one else in all the world can be who only you can be. No one else in all the world can do what only you can do. If you want to get excited about life and if you want to be motivated to become the best person you can be, start there. Allow God to show you who He created you to be. Allow God to show you what He created you to do. Start there, and that will be the beginning of the right kind of dream.

The most important thing I have learned in my years of life, is that the entire world has been created to function in a God-centered way. God created this world and He has something in mind for it. So, it makes sense to me, that life will naturally work out best if I learn what God has in mind, and begin to cooperate with that. For me, that means that God comes first. God is to be at the center of life, with everything else ordered around that. Everything else in life derives its meaning and direction from that vital center. After all, the first commandment demands it: "Thou shalt have no other gods before me." God first. Jesus put God first, too. When someone asked him about the greatest commandment, he said, "You shall love the Lord, your God with all your heart, with all you mind, with all your soul, and with all your strength." That's first. Put God first, and you will receive what you need to become the unique and wonderful person God planned you to be. Put God first, and then you will know what dreams to pursue.

Then, as you formulate your dreams, people have to come next. Jesus said, "Love God with all your heart" first. But next, he said, "You shall love your neighbor as yourself." I'm here to tell you that the self-centered life is an automatically unhappy life. That's the danger of the picture Bloody Mary was painting for Joe Cable and Liat. That circle of love and concern just wasn't big enough. Like the man who prayed: "God bless me and my wife, my son John and his wife, us four and no more". That's too small a circle. There must be more to life than the pursuit of personal happiness.

No, if you want to be unhappy, just make happiness your primary dream. Happiness will never be found by looking for it. Happiness is a serendipity. You seek something bigger, something more important, and then happiness is thrown in for good measure. That's the only way it comes. I remember something Albert Schweitzer said to a graduating class. He said: "The only ones among you who will be really happy will be those who have sought and found how to serve." Of course.

Is there something you can do with your life which will make the world a better place? Is there something you can do with your life which will make other people glad that they are alive and that they have come to know you? Something that will make people stand a little taller, walk a little straighter, have their hearts a little happier. I like something Horace Mann once said. Horace Mann is sometimes called the father of American education. He said, "Be ashamed to die until you have won some victory for humanity."

Something like that is a dream that is worthy of you. It is a dream that will call forth the best from within you, and give you the deepest satisfaction and the greatest happiness. Know that you are never alone as you reach for the best in life. God, who is the giver of dreams, is always with us, and He will give us all we need to make our dreams come true.

So, don't miss it. Make sure you have a dream for your life. And make sure that your dream is big enough to be worthy of you. Just remember: "You've got to have a dream. If you don't have a dream, how're you going to have a dream come true?"

Prayer: Give us a dream, O God, Your dream for our lives. Make it a dream big enough to excite us, motivate us, and call forth the best from within us. Give us a dream, and then give us all we need to make our dream come true. We pray with gratitude for all Your love and goodness to us. In Jesus' name. Amen.

You've Got To Be Carefully Taught

Matthew 18:1-14

One source of beautiful music in "South Pacific" is the two romances that are developing simultaneously. Nurse Nellie Forbush and Emile deBecque fall in love first. She sings, "I'm in love with a wonderful guy." And he sings, "Some enchanted evening, you may see a stranger, you may see a stranger across a crowded room, and somehow you know, you know even then, that somewhere you'll see her again and again... Once you have found her, never let her go." It's beautiful, and it's become a classic, romantic ballad.

And, there is another romance in "South Pacific." Lieutenant Joe Cable falls in love with a beautiful young Tonkanese girl named Liat. Again, it's a beautiful romance, and Joe describes Liat in song as "Younger than springtime, softer than starlight, lovely as laughter." I suppose love makes you say beautiful things like that. Liat's mother, Bloody Mary has promoted the romance, because she wants Joe for her son-in-law. One day, as she was describing the wonderful life they would have together on the island, she says, "The first moment I see you I know you are right man for Liat, and she is right girl for you. You have special good babies!" Hearing that, immediately fear grips him. The thought of children born of their relationship sends Joe into a panic. He says that he cannot marry Liat, and he leaves. That beautiful, romantic relationship has crumbled.

In the meanwhile, the romance between Nellie Forbush and Emile deBecque falls into problems of its own. One night, Emile introduces Nellie to two Polynesian children. She assumes that they belong to one of the servants, and she is enchanted by them. But when he tells her that they are his children and that their mother was his Polynesian wife who had died years before, something grips her. Prejudice comes slithering out from under a rock, and she begins to cry. She makes an excuse about an appointment she has forgotten, and leaves, quickly and awkwardly.

For several days she avoids him and refuses his calls. Then Joe Cable and Nellie are together, talking about life back home in the U.S. Emile approaches them and says, "Nellie, I must see you. You have asked for a transfer. Why? What does it mean?" "I'll talk to you tomorrow," she says. "No, now!" he replies, "What does it mean, Nellie?"

"It means I can't marry you. Do you understand? I can't marry you!" "Because of my children?" "O no, not your children. They're sweet." "It's their Polynesian mother, then, their mother who died." "Yes. I can't help it. It isn't as if I can give you a good reason. There is no reason. It's emotional. This is something that is born in me." Emphatically, Emile says, "It is not! I do not believe this is born in you." "Then why?" she asks. "Why do I feel the way I do? All I know is, I can't help it. I can't help it. Joe, Joe, explain how we feel." And she runs away in tears.

Emile turns to Joe and asks, "What makes her talk like that? I do not believe it is born in you. I do not believe it!" Joe says, "It's not born in you. It happens to you after you are born." And he begins to sing...

> "You've got to be taught to hate and fear, you've got to
> be taught from year to year,
> It's got to be drummed in your dear little ear, you've
> got to be carefully taught.
> You've got to be taught to be afraid of people whose
> eyes are oddly made,
> And people whose skin is a different shade, you've got
> to be carefully taught.
> You've got to be taught before it's too late, before you
> are six or seven or eight,

> To hate all the people your relatives hate, you've got to
> be carefully taught."

Nellie Forbush and Joe Cabel had been taught some wrong things, and they had some unlearning to do. As I often say in classes I teach, "Most significant adult learning requires some unlearning." I am happy to say that they were successful in their unlearning. They discovered that love is more powerful than prejudice, and Nellie's love for Emile and Joe's love for Liat won out, and their love was beautiful. But, right now, our focus is on being carefully taught.

When we read the scriptures, we discover that there were two things that made Jesus really angry. One was when a person profaned that which is holy. The second was when a person hurt someone who was weak or vulnerable, especially children.

Clearly, Jesus loved children. Jesus cared about children. In fact, in the scripture cited at the beginning of this chapter, Jesus even used child-likeness as a quality essential for entrance into the Kingdom of Heaven. He pointed out that there is so much we can learn from children: their willingness to trust, their quickness to forgive, their wide-eyed curiosity about life, their endless "Why?" questions, their capacity for wonder and excitement, their openness, their energy, and their desire to learn. Yes, we would all do well to be more child-like.

But, the very things that are so admirable about children can also be their weakness. We all come into this world as incomplete persons. We are little bundles of potential, but we are incomplete. We have to learn, and grow, and mature. And, in that process, especially in the beginning, we are like sponges, eager to absorb whatever information, attitudes, values, or behaviors that come our way. And that's why Jesus says that we all have a particular responsibility in helping others grow up to maturity. We'd better help and not hurt. We'd better ease their way and not put a stumbling block in their path. Jesus said, "It is not the will of your Father in heaven that even one of these little ones should be lost." In fact, in some of the strongest language ever heard coming from the mouth of Jesus, he said, "If any of you put a stumbling block before one of these little ones, it would be better for you if a great millstone were fastened around your neck and you were drowned in the depth of the sea." It's true. Every person has to be taught. We will do much of the teaching, so we had better be very careful to teach all the right things. So much depends upon that.

During my growing up years, I was taught many good things. And I will always be grateful for that. But I was also taught some wrong things. And when, as an adult, I learned that I had been taught much that was wrong, I was embarrassed about that, even angry about that. Those older should have known better. They should have taught me more carefully.

I grew up in a world where black people and white people were separated. We went to separate schools, ate in separate restaurants, stayed in separate hotels, used separate rest rooms, and drank out of separate drinking fountains. That's the way it was. My culture taught me that that's the way it was supposed to be. I was taught so well that I was in high school before it occurred to me to question any of that and I was embarrassed that I had been so morally blind. And I was angry that those teaching me had done it so carefully and so well.

Nellie Forbush and Joe Cable had been carefully taught as well. Even when their minds told them that their feelings were off base, the feelings were still there to be dealt with. They didn't fully understand them, perhaps didn't even want them, but they were still there, shaping their attitudes and their behavior.

As I said, I was taught some very good things. I well remember mornings in Sunday school, singing, "Jesus loves the little children, all the children of the world; red and yellow, black and white, they are precious in his sight; Jesus loves the little children of the world." I was taught that in Sunday school. But why did no one teach me about the inconsistency between what we sang about in Sunday school and what we did every day?

Do you wonder, as I do, what we are teaching our children and our grandchildren every day? Not the things we teach when we are *trying* to teach, but those more powerful lessons we teach when we *don't know* we are teaching. Do you worry, as I do, lest we teach them things today that they will become embarrassed about or even angry about later in life? Don't underestimate it! Every moment of every day our children are learning. They are learning about what is important in life. They are learning about what they think will make them happy and fulfilled. They are learning how to value or devalue people. They are learning about what behaviors are acceptable or unacceptable. And they are learning much of that from us. We'd better be careful about what we are teaching them. Those little sponges are watching us, and they are learning the most powerful lessons when we least expect it.

I remember hearing about a family who went to the beach, laid out their beach towels, and set up their umbrella. Then, the father had to go back to the car to get something. He walked along the sand and left his footprints there. Shortly thereafter, his kindergarten son started out to follow him. And there he was, stretching out his little legs, trying to make his feet fall into his father's footsteps.

That's happening in your family. It's happening in your neighborhood. You are a role model for someone. They're watching you. And they're trying with all their might to live up to or down to the standards you are setting. We have no choice about that. We are influences either for good or for ill. We either make this world a better place or a less noble place because of the quality of life we live. And we can't just decide we don't want the responsibility.

Do you remember the statement from Charles Barkley, star NBA basketball player? He said, "I'm a basketball player. I'm not a role model." But he is. He doesn't have a choice. Every moment of every day, by the way he lives his life, he is teaching. We all are. And we had all better be careful about what we teach. Jesus said, "Don't be a stumbling block." Whatever you do, don't be a stumbling block!

It's so sinister. With the best of intentions we pass out good advice, *good advice*, and then that good advice is cancelled out by having our actions observed. And those who look at us say, "What you do speaks so loudly I can't hear a word you're saying."

Surely we know by now that the old phrase, "Pay attention to what I say, not what I do" – that doesn't wash.

I remember a good friend of ours telling us about the concern her adult children were feeling for the bad language their children were picking up at school. One night this grandmother was baby-sitting and her granddaughter came out with one of those words. The grandmother said, "That's not a nice word to use. Where did you hear that?" With all the innocence of childhood, the little girl said, "That's what Crocodile Dundee says." The parents were blaming the school, yet all the while the little sponge was soaking up the language from a video mom and dad had rented and were showing at home! It's true. At every moment of every day we are teaching, for good or for ill, whether we want to or not. We teach by the living of our lives. Jesus said, "Be careful!"

Of course, the good news is that if people can learn negative, destructive, life negating things from us, they can also learn positive, constructive, life affirming things from us as well. And what's more, God is at work in that direction every moment of every day, even while we are asleep! As Jesus said, God is out searching for every lost sheep, so that no one need be lost. What a marvelous privilege it is for us to be co-workers with God, teaching all the right things, helping to shape lives in right directions. I can't think of anything more important than that!

I've been preaching for over 50 years now. I've been pastor of a number of churches. I've officiated at countless weddings and funerals. I've taught innumerable classes. I've preached thousands of sermons. But I've never had a responsibility in life more important than being a father and a grandfather, and being a friend and good example to children. And it has been my constant prayer that those looking at me would not have to unlearn wrong things they learned from me, that their lives would not be made more difficult and painful because of the example I set, and that they would not have to climb over stumbling blocks I put in their way!

What a marvelous opportunity we have! We can help children and youth grow up knowing that they are loved, that their lives are of infinite worth because they are the sons and daughters of God. We can assure that they are secure and have a sense of well being because this is God's world and He is for us and not against us. We can teach that all of us who share planet earth are brothers and sisters because we are all children of the same Father, and that there are ways of living that are better than other ways of living because God loves us. He does not want us to hurt other people and He doesn't want us to hurt ourselves.

I can't think of a greater gift you can give anyone than to teach them all of that. And, of course, God wants every one of His children to have that gift. That's what Jesus was getting at when he said, "I have come that you may have life, and have it abundantly!"

Of course, the best place for all of that to happen is in the home and in the Church. And, I have to tell you, I get a kick out of seeing so many children and youth running around the church, going to classes, eating in the fellowship hall, singing and playing games, coming to worship, and smiling all the while. They look like they feel at home in church. What a gift - to be a child of God, happy, and at home in God's world.

You can help make that happen. You can do it as a parent, as a grandparent, or as a friend. And, you can do it as a teacher. I would love to see an army of committed Christians signing up to teach. Not just a trickle, but an army! I assure you: there are not many causes to which you can give yourself that will yield more satisfying dividends!

Let me pull it all together with this closing image: a little fellow was in Sunday school, as he was every week. His teacher asked him a question. She asked, "How is it that you became a Christian?" He shrugged his shoulders and said, "I don't know. I guess it just runs in our family!"

The song says, "You have to be carefully taught". Teach that!

Prayer: Loving God, our Father, we sense the awesome responsibility which is ours. We dare not attempt it without Your help. So, as we live our lives among those who are watching us, let us help and not hurt. Help us to build up and not tear down. Help us to ennoble life and not demean it. Help us to love and to give as Jesus did. For it is in his name that we pray. Amen.

This Nearly Was Mine

Luke 18:18-23

In the previous chapter, we noted a sad chapter in the "South Pacific" story. Joe Cable had told Liat that he could not marry her, even though he loved her and was deliriously happy with her; but, he was Caucasian and she was Tonkanese, and he had been carefully taught. And Nellie Forbush had told Emile de Becque that she could not marry him, even though she loved him and wanted to be with him; but he had once married a Polynesian woman and had had children with her. And Nellie, too, had been carefully taught.

Both Joe and Nellie had been taught by their cultures who they could associate with, and who they could not, who they could love and who they could not, who they could marry and who they could not. They had been carefully taught. But what they had been taught was not making them happy. Indeed, it was getting in the way of their happiness. It's tragic, isn't it, when we are taught wrong things, and taught them so well.

You remember that Joe Cable had been sent to the island to recruit Emile de Becque to go with him on a dangerous reconnaissance mission. Initially, Emile refused, because he was in love with Nellie and wanted to spend the rest of his life with her. The mission was dangerous - he might be killed - and he had so much to live for. But, when Nellie told him that she could not marry him, he was devastated. He had less to live for, so, he agreed to go on the dangerous, life threatening mission. Joe and Emile went, they performed heroically, and they made a significant contribution to the war effort in the Pacific.

But before going on that mission, Joe had some time to think. He loved Liat, yet he had told her that he couldn't marry her! What kind of man would do that? What kind of stupid man would do that? So, before leaving on the mission he had a change of heart. He loved Liat, he wanted to be with her, she wanted to be with him, and so, in spite of what he had been taught, he was ready to commit to love and life with Liat.

Just after he sang his song, "You've Got To Be Carefully Taught," Joe turned to Emile and said, "You've got the right idea, de Becque, living here on this island. If I get out of this alive, I'm gonna stay right here. Everything I care about is right here." Emile replies: "If all you care about is here, this is a good place to be. When all you care about is taken away from you, there is no good place. I came so close to it, so close..." And he begins to sing...

"One dream in my heart, one love to be living for,
One love to be living for, this nearly was mine.
One girl for my dream, one partner in paradise,
This promise of paradise, this nearly was mine.
Close to my heart she came, only to fly away,
Only to fly as day flies from moonlight.
Now, now I'm alone, still dreaming of paradise,
Still saying that paradise once nearly was mine."

Before going on with this chapter, I have to finish the "South Pacific"story. As I said, Joe Cable and Emile de Becque went on the reconnaissance mission, performed heroically, and made a significant contribution to the war effort in the Pacific. I'm glad that we learned that Joe had a change of heart. He had decided to return to the island and marry Liat. I'm sure they would have been happy together. But, tragically, he was killed on the mission and his loving plans were not carried out.

In the meanwhile, Nellie Forbush was doing a lot of thinking as well, and a lot of unlearning. She decided to follow her heart, so if Emile returned from the dangerous mission, she would be there, waiting for him. They had been told that he was missing and might even be dead. Well, you know what happened, as it happens so often on Broadway. In one of the most heart-warming scenes of the musical, Nellie was there, at Emile's home with his two children, loving them, and enjoying being with them. It was as close to Emile as she could be at that moment. The children were teaching her the song they had loved to sing with their father: "Dites-moi, Pourquoi, La vie est belle, Dites-moi, Pourquoi," And just at that moment, Emile appeared and joined in the song, "La vie est gai." Of course they all embraced, Nellie, Emile, and the two children all joined in a group hug. And, I am sure Nellie and Emile went on to marry and live happily ever after! Such is the way of the musicals we all love!

But right now, I want us to return to that moment Emile thought he had lost it all. He said, "I came so close, so close." That's one of the really tragic moments of life: to be so close to something we want, something we have dreamed about and longed for, to be so close we can taste it, but it slips through our fingers. How tragic!

Perhaps it is professional: you wanted a job or a position so badly, you knew you could do it, you worked hard for it, and you deserved it, but it was given to someone else. That hurts, doesn't it? Perhaps it has to do with family: you wanted only the best for your children. You did the best you knew, and it all started out so well. But somewhere along the way things began to go wrong, their life took a wrong direction, and now they are hurting, and as a result you are hurting. It could have turned out so well, but it didn't, at least not so far. Or, perhaps, as with Emile, it is relational. Perhaps you were in love, really in love, but your love was not returned. It hurts, doesn't it, to be rejected? Or, perhaps you were married. Maybe you thought everything was okay, but one day your spouse asked for a divorce, and your life took a turn you didn't expect - a turn you didn't want.

The thing that makes our experience doubly painful is that we had a taste of it. If we had not gotten that close, we would never know what we had missed. But to experience some of it, a taste of it, and then to have it taken away, that hurts. I suspect all of us have had such experiences of disappointment, experiences of loss, when we felt like singing, "This nearly was mine." This dream, this promise, this hope, it was nearly mine.

That was the experience of the young man who came to Jesus that day. He was a fine young man, a good young man. There was much about him to admire, and he wanted many of the right things. In fact, he came to Jesus asking, "What must I do to inherit eternal life?" Of course, we know that, in the gospels, eternal life is not just a quantity of years, it is also a quality of years. So, this young man wanted the very best in life. He didn't want anything good to pass him by. I give him high marks for that.

But have you noticed how Jesus, again and again, cuts through all the fluff to get to the main point? After the young man told Jesus he had kept the commandments, Jesus saw how attached he was to "things." "Things" were more important to him than anything else. So, Jesus said, "Go and sell all that you have and give it to the poor and then come and follow me." Hearing this, the scripture says, he became sad, because he was very rich. He wanted to follow Jesus, be clear about that. He really wanted to follow Jesus, but not as much as he wanted his money, his things, his stuff. He came so close. He asked the right questions. And he wanted it; he wanted it, but just not enough to make the full commitment. And, he went away sad. I'm sure he spent the rest of his life sad. And, he too could sing, "This nearly was mine."

Do you remember when the Apostle Paul was in prison at Caesarea Maritima? There in that dramatic moment, he appeared before Festus and then before King Agrippa. They had the power of life and death over him. But, setting aside his own safety, he did what he so often did. He told them the Christian story. He poured out his heart to them. And Agrippa said, "You almost persuade me to be a Christian – almost." But not quite. Just think about who he could have become, just think about what he could have done, this King. If only he had said, "Yes." When he felt the impulse, when God was tugging at his heart, if only he had said, "Yes," what a difference it would have made. He would have spent his life making a positive difference in the world, being happy and fulfilled and productive. But, instead, he spent the rest of his life just a hollow man, just a shadow of what might have been. He, too, could sing, "This nearly was mine."

The world is full of people like that. Even churches are full of people like that. So close, but not quite. They have felt God's tug at their lives. They have been attracted to all the promises, and to all the possibilities of authentic discipleship. They have even gotten a taste of what it feels like to bask in the warmth of God's love, to feel like they are somebody, to enlist in a significant task, and to know that their lives are what the are supposed to be. To get a taste of that, and then, at the last moment to draw back, to refuse to make the commitment, and then to plod through every day, knowing who we ought to be, knowing what we ought to do, knowing, but not doing. Almost, but not quite. How sad.

It reminds me of a story my father told about his childhood. He and some friends were out playing "follow the leader." The leader would jump over a stump and everyone would jump over the stump. The leader would climb over a fence and everyone would climb over the fence. The leader would get a running start and leap over a creek. Most of them jumped over the creek. But my father got his running start, and just as he was getting ready to jump, someone shouted, "Stop!". And he sort of jumped, and he sort of didn't. So, he landed in the middle of the creek.

I know so many people like that. They sort of jump into the Christian life and they sort of don't. And, the result is, they have the worst of all worlds. They are too Christian to enjoy sin, but they are too sinful to make the final commitment. So they are left dreaming of paradise, and thinking of what it would have been like to be an authentic follower of Jesus, but left singing, "This nearly was mine."

Recently I was reading about a young priest who was assigned to his first parish. Sunday came and he was preparing for his first Mass. He looked out at the parking lot and saw a great many cars there, and people streaming into the church. He thought to himself, "Wonderful, we will have a great crowd today!" But when he went into the sanctuary, there was only a handful of people there. The next week the same thing happened: many cars, people streaming into the church, but only a handful for Mass. So, he decided to investigate. The next Sunday he followed people into the church, and found that they were coming in, dipping their hands in holy water, making the sign of the cross, then turning around and leaving to attend to other things.

I see that far too much: people content to sprinkle holy water around instead of seriously following Jesus; people content to paddle around in the shallows instead of diving in head first to commitment; people "sort of" jumping and "sort of" not. They feel the call. They sense God's pull. And they want to commit, but for some reason they pull back, and spend the rest of their lives singing "This nearly was mine."

I vividly remember my experience in the outdoor pavilion at McComb, Mississippi, the night I made my first serious Christian commitment. I remember that as clearly as if it were yesterday. I sensed God's presence. I felt God's pull at my life. I heard God's call, and I said

"Yes." What I want you to hear loud and clear is that I have never for one moment regretted the decision I made there that night. I have not always been faithful to it, but it's made all the difference. I shudder to think what my life would be like if I had not said "Yes."

To wander around aimlessly, not really knowing what life is about; to be, like the rich young man who came to Jesus that day, caring more about "things" than about people; to care more about "stuff" than about eternal purpose; to be unsure of my worth and every day attempt that impossible task of trying to prove my worth to myself and others; I can't think of any greater hell than that: to feel that I will be unloved and unworthy until I prove that I deserve all of that. To live like that is to be like Sisyphus, forever pushing the boulder up the mountain. Just when you almost reach the top it rolls back down the mountain and you have to start over again, year after exhausting year, pushing that boulder up the mountain. It is so exhausting, so discouraging, and so impossible, to have to prove your worth, to have to earn love from God and from others. I think about all of that and I have to say, "That could have been my life," that kind of empty, pointless, frustrating life could have been mine if Christ had not called to me, touched me with his amazing grace, and I said "Yes!"

I don't know where you are right now in your Christian commitment. That's between you and God. But, if you haven't made the commitment, don't miss it. It's never too late. Don't be content to dabble in holy water. Don't settle for "sort of" jumping. Don't spend the rest of your life looking back in regret and singing, "This nearly was mine." How much better to reach out with hands of faith and take hold of all that God wants to give: life, abundant life, now and for eternity.

That's what William Booth did. Do you know the name William Booth? You should, because he is the founder of the Salvation Army. The time came in his life when God became real for him. God reached out to him, called to him, and he said "Yes." After he made that commitment, he lived a remarkable life of love and compassion, especially toward the poor of London. He said, about his experience, "Once I got the poor of London on my heart, I decided that God would have all of William Booth there is!" And the Salvation Army is the result.

Do you hear that? "I decided that God would have all of William Booth there is!" Not just part of him. Not just "almost" making a commitment. Not just splashing a little holy water around. Not sort of jumping and sort of not. All of William Booth there is - All.

God has given His all to His children. He asks no less of us. I pray that we will be so touched by God's grace that we will make a new commitment here and now. As the hymn says, "All to Jesus I surrender; all to him I freely give." Either that, or we will spend the rest of our days singing, "This nearly was mine."

Prayer: Loving Father, You have given us so much. Help us to respond to Your generosity by giving ourselves to you. Make our response not half-hearted, tentative, partial, but a commitment of all that we are and all that we have. In Jesus' name, who gave his all for us. Amen.

Singing in the Rain

2 Corinthians 5:17-20

Several years ago, Patricia and I saw a stage production of "Singing in the Rain" at the Orpheum Theater in Memphis, Tennessee. Earlier we had seen the movie starring Gene Kelly, Debbie Reynolds, and Donald O'Connor. The movie contains some of the classic singing and dancing scenes on film. Because we had loved the film, we eagerly anticipated seeing the stage version.

The story is about two vaudeville entertainers, Don Lockwood and his sidekick, Cosmo Brown, who had never made it to the big time. They played minor venues and were anything but stars. They decided to try their luck in Hollywood during the silent picture era – talkies had not yet begun. Initially their luck did not change. Still, they were out there on the fringes, hanging on by their fingernails, hoping for a break. One day, they were off-screen, unimportant helpers in the filming of a movie, when several of the stunt men were injured. They were about to cancel that day's filming and the director was frantic. So, Don Lockwood volunteered to do the stunt work. As it turned out, he was good at it, so he received several more opportunities. The producer was so impressed with him that he decided to make him a leading man, playing opposite an established silent film star named Lina Lamont. Lina was a beauty, and just made to order for silent pictures, because she had a horrible voice that grated on the nerves! Whether she was speaking or singing, her voice gave one the same feeling as a fingernail being scraped across a chalk board. But, that was okay, because she was a star of silent pictures.

Don Lockwood and Lina Lamont were a big hit together. As their pictures made money they became bigger and bigger stars. Then, a rival studio made the first talking movie, "The Jazz Singer," and suddenly everything changed. They, too, had to make the transition to sound!

They decided to make a musical. When they first showed it to a test audience, it was an absolute disaster. No one could stand the grating voice of Lina Lamont. Everyone at the studio was in a panic. What to do? How to solve the problem? Then they hit upon an idea: there was a beautiful young actress, singer, and dancer in the chorus named Kathy Selden. They decided to have her be the speaking and singing voice. Lina Lamont could provide the famous and familiar star face, and Kathy Selden could be the voice they recorded. Of course, the picture then was a marvelous hit.

I won't tell you how the whole thing turns out, but predictably, Don Lockwood falls in love with Kathy Selden…head-over-heels, out of his skull, hopelessly, and helplessly in love. One night, after they had shared a wonderful evening, he took her home. He was caught up in the beautiful, powerful emotion of love. As he was leaving, it started to rain. But it didn't matter to him. He was oblivious to it. The rain was pouring down, he was getting drenched, but he didn't care. He sang and danced all over the stage because he was in love. Let's listen to his song:

"I'm singing in the rain, just singing in the rain. What a glorious feeling, I'm happy again. I'm laughing at clouds so dark up above, the sun's in my heart and I'm ready for love. Let the stormy clouds chase everyone from the place, Come on with the rain, I've a smile on my face.

I'll walk down the lane with a happy refrain, and singing, just singing in the rain."

We look at that scene and we think, "He's crazy! He's crazy to be dancing around and singing in the rain!" I suppose that when you are in love you are a little crazy. The fact is, Don Lockwood was so much in love that night, so caught up in the crazy feelings of it, that he didn't mind the rain. Maybe he didn't even notice it. At least for that moment, his love was so powerful that it overwhelmed everything negative in his life!

Remember that scene. Remember Don Lockwood singing and dancing in the rain, and you will remember a basic principle in life: the mind cannot focus on more than one thing at a time. Whatever you are focusing on pushes everything else out of your consciousness. For example, if you are worried, it is difficult to concentrate on your work. If you are in pain, it is difficult to be creative. If you are tormented by a compulsion, it is difficult to think good thoughts. If you are angry, it is difficult to be at peace. Whatever emotion, sensation, thought, or compulsion is more powerful will push everything else from our minds.

Since that is true, it suggests that many of our approaches to life's problems have been off base. Often, when you focus on the problem, instead of solving it, you give it more power. The more you think about it, the more it grips you. I believe that the best way to deal with problems is to turn our attention to something more positive and give it the power. I saw a cartoon depicting two teen-aged girls walking down the street. Across the street, walking toward them, was a teen-aged boy. One girl nudged the other, saying with a giggle, "There's Jeffrey!" The second girl replied, "Don't pay him any attention. We're not seeing each other any more. I haven't spoken to him for three days, six hours, and twenty-seven minutes!" I must say, she isn't likely to get over Jeffrey by counting the minutes since they talked. That gives the failed relationship more power over her. If she wants to get over Jeffrey, she will need to give her attention to George, Gary, or Fred.

In attempting to help youth resist gangs and drugs, many have said to them, "Just say 'No!'" I am in favor of saying, "No!" to the destructive impulses of life, but probably something more is needed. Why not put a positive in place of that negative influence? Why not provide good schools, stable families, exciting after school activities such as sports, music, or Boys and Girls Clubs? Why not insure some interesting jobs? Let a positive replace the negative.

I've seen the principle at work for years in counseling. A person comes to see me and he has a problem. He is obsessed with the problem. Hour after hour, day after day, he rehearses the problem, not letting go. He keeps picking at the scabs of the problem until he has it bleeding again. The more he focuses on the problem, the more power he gives it. As long as he is focusing on the problem, he is not able to reach out for the resources of faith.

Very often we religious people attempt to overcome negative influences simply by "trying harder." We say, "Don't do that. Don't think about that." I talked about that in the chapter on "My Favorite Things," suggesting that we try not to think about the color black. We discovered that the harder we try not to think about black, the more we think about black. By concentrating on it, we give it more power. I proposed that, instead of trying not to think black, we think about red. While we are thinking about red, we are not thinking of black.

That's the way it works. Think red, forget about black. Think Fred, forget about Jeffrey. Think love, forget about the rain.

The scripture from 2 Corinthians makes the same point. Listen: "If anyone is in Christ there is a new creation: everything old has passed away; see, everything has become new!" For Christians, a relationship with Christ is not something tacked on out there at the periphery of life, like some pleasant additive or some desirable extra. The relationship with Christ is not a foot-note or an afterthought. No, for us Christ is at the center of life, and there at the center, he begins to push out everything that doesn't belong there. That's how everything becomes new: the old is shoved aside and all life is created anew. Life is re-ordered. All our values and priorities are rearranged because something new is now at the center of life – Christ!

Is there something old that is messing up your life? Old guilt, old painful memories, old resentments or anger, old compulsions or temptations? You don't remove their power over you just by dealing with them. You have to replace them with something better and more powerful. There cannot be a void at the center of life. Something is going to be there; if not Christ, then something else. What I have been saying for over fifty years now is that only Christ is worthy of that important position. Only Christ at the center of life can make life abundant. Even if you manage to push something negative out, unless you fill that void with something better, another negative will rush right in to take its place. Jesus told us about a house that was cleared of demons, but because it was left empty, even more powerful demons moved in to replace the first. Hear me: it's not enough to struggle against the negative, life destroying elements of life. You've got to make sure that there is a more powerful, life-giving presence at the center of life. That presence fills the void and keeps the destructive forces at bay. As a Christian, I believe that the best central presence is Christ.

Keep Christ in the center

In his letter to the Corinthians, Paul declares that when we are "in Christ" all of life is made new. The old is put aside and the new is created. How does Christ do that for us? To begin with, Christ assures us that we are the sons and daughters of God, known and loved by the Father. We are loved absolutely, thoroughly, continually, and unconditionally. We experience the extent of the Father's love at Jesus' crucifixion. Nowhere else do we see the great heart of God so clearly revealed as there at the cross. There we experience God's love becoming vulnerable and willing to suffer for us. That is how we distinguish real love from its counterfeit expressions. Authentic love becomes vulnerable and pours itself out on behalf of the loved one. Once we experience that and really *know* that we are loved like that, it changes us and everything becomes new.

Further, when Christ is there at the center of life, he shows us the path to authentic life. He shows us how to live it fully, abundantly, and joyfully. He reconciles us with others, helping us to embrace them as our brothers and sisters, and helping us to be gracious and giving toward them. He assures us that we are never alone, that he is always with us and that his grace is sufficient for us, seeing us through and providing for us in every life situation. With that assurance, there is nothing that can defeat us, nothing that can destroy us. That is the promise, as long as we allow Christ to re-create life day after day with him at the center. That is the way it works!

In the early part of the nineteenth century, Thomas Chalmers wrote a sermon which has become a classic. He entitled it, "The Expulsive Power of a New Affection." The thing he stressed was that when the pains, problems, and perplexities of life come along, we don't just try harder. We don't just pretend they aren't there. We don't just spray around a little deodorant cover up. Instead, we reach out in faith to take hold of something better, stronger, and more life-giving. We take hold of Christ. And, with Christ at the center of life, the destructive forces are displaced and expelled! I like his title, don't you? "The Expulsive Power of a New Affection" – Christ!

If you want that to happen in your life, the place to start is by believing it can happen. Then, make this prayer your own: "God, beginning now, I place my trust in Christ, and in Christ alone. Take Your rightful place at the center of my life, and expel all the things that don't belong there." When you pray that prayer sincerely it marks the beginning of new life.

One of the best examples of what I have been writing about is found in the gospel of Luke. Jesus' disciples were in a boat on the Sea of Galilee when a terrible storm began to form and they were terrified. Jesus, concerned about these men he loved so much, began to walk to them on the water. Peter recognized him and stepped out of the boat to meet him. As long as he kept his eyes on Jesus, he was okay. But, as he began to feel the blowing of the wind, he began to experience the fury of the storm. He looked around him, and he became afraid. He took his eyes off Jesus, concentrated on the storm, and he began to sink.

He had to choose where his focus would be: on the storm or on Jesus. He couldn't do both at once, and everything depended upon his choice. Do you hear the truth in that? When he looked again at Jesus, Jesus took him by the hand, and he got into the boat with Jesus. What a beautiful picture of faith – to get into the boat with Jesus. And the scripture says that when Peter got into the boat with Jesus, the storm subsided!

That is exactly what I have been attempting to write. Place Christ at the center, get into the boat with Jesus, and the storms of life lose much of their power. You will discover that, there in the boat with Jesus, you are equal to any storm life sends your way. You may even find yourself singing and dancing in the rain. "If anyone is in Christ, there is a new creation: everything old has passed away; see, everything has become new!"

Prayer: God, our Father, help us to love You enough to give You Your rightful place at the center of life. Help us to love You enough to love You above all else. Help us to trust Your promise to make all life new. Help us to love You with such a powerful affection, that it will expel the negative forces from our lives forever. We pray in the name of Christ, who makes all things new. Amen.

Whistle a Happy Tune

Mark 9:14-27

"The King and I" is another of the Broadway musicals with a light hearted mood, a happy ending, and a number of sing-able and memorable tunes. The story is about a widow from England who was hired as a teacher for the children of the King of Siam. She boarded a boat with her son, Louie, and set sail for this land across the sea. They had just anchored in the port of Bangkok when the captain looked through his telescope and saw a boat load of soldiers coming out to meet them. The person leading them was second in command in all of Siam. The little boy, Louie, asked if he could look. He took the telescope and when he looked, he gasped. He turned to his mother and said, "They look so cruel! (But) father would not have liked us to be afraid, would he?" His mother replied, "No Louie, father would not have liked us to be afraid. Not ever!" He looked at his mother and asked, "Doesn't anything ever frighten you, mother?" "O yes, sometimes," she said. "Well, what do you do?" he asked. She smiled and said, "I whistle!" "O, that's why you whistle?" "Uh huh," she said, "that's why I whistle." And she begins to sing…

> "Whenever I feel afraid, I hold my head erect, and
>   whistle a happy tune so no one will suspect I'm
>   afraid.

> While shivering in my shoes I strike a careless pose and
>   whistle a happy tune and no one ever knows I'm
>   afraid.
> The result of this deception is very strange to tell, for
>   when I fool the people I fear, I fool myself as well.
> I whistle a happy tune and every single time the
>   happiness in the tune convinces me that I'm not
>   afraid.
> Make believe you're brave and the trick will take you
>   far…
> You may be as brave as you make believe you are!
>   (Whistle)
> You may be as brave as you make believe you are!"

When she concludes her song, Louie says, "I think that's a good idea, mother. A very good idea!" I agree with Louie. It is a good idea, but it goes beyond the whistling. There is more to it than that. That is why we have to have a chapter about it.

What do you do in the fearful times of life? We all have them, you know. As someone has said, "In our kind of world, you either have to be a little afraid, or a little stupid." So, the question is not whether or not you will sometimes be afraid. The question is, how do you handle the fear when it comes?

The method Louie's mother used is a good one. When she was afraid, she whistled a happy tune. In other words, she acted as if she was not afraid. And, by acting as if she was not afraid, that very act helped rid her of her fear. Did you notice those very significant words of her song? "The result of this deception is very strange to tell; for when I fool the people I fear, I fool myself as well. I whistle a happy tune and every single time the happiness in the tune convinces me that I'm not afraid." That is an important principle: by acting as if she were not afraid, something happened within her to remove her fear.

That principle has become increasingly important to me through the years, so I talk about it more and more in my writing, preaching, and teaching. This is the essence of it:

If you want faith, you act *as if* you have faith. It is in the *acting as if* that faith comes.

Every week I encounter people who are looking for faith. In effect they say, "Prove the Christian faith to me and then I will try it." Of course, that is the very thing no one can do. No one can prove the truth of the Christian faith to anyone before they try it. There is much persuasive evidence, but not irresistible evidence, so I don't offer proof. However, consider this: we have all discovered a great many paths in life that don't lead us where we want to go. We have looked for life in a great many places where we have not found it. There are many shiny, glittering things that call to us, promising so much and delivering so little. We've been led down that path before, haven't we? We know about that God-shaped empty place at the center of life. As long as that place is not filled with the experience of God, we are lonely, anxious, restless, and homesick – you supply your own descriptive word, but you know the feeling, don't you? We have tried many things and none have worked very well.

In the midst of our search for a life that works, we encounter some people whose lives are admirable. They seem to have "put it all together." They are examples of the kind of authentic humanness we admire, and we know that whatever they have, we want. They tell us that their faith is what makes a difference in their lives. So, on the basis of that, we reach out for faith. After hearing the request for proof so many times, finally I have learned to say in response, "I can't prove it to you, but try living your life *as if* what the Christian faith says is true. Allow God to prove it in your own experience, because experiential proof is the only proof there is. The validation is in *our experience* of a life made new and abundant because we have begun to live by faith."

Early in my ministry, I would attempt to persuade seekers by logical argument. There is, after all, much persuasive evidence available. I remember a very bright college student I took on as a project. I tried one argument and then another, but in his facile mind, he could always find a counter argument that was persuasive for him. Finally, in frustration, I said to him, "I can't prove it to you. All I know to say is that my life has been different and better since I have begun to live by faith." He looked at me with a surprised look on his face and replied, "That's the most convincing argument I have ever heard!"

It is the principle of "living as if." You begin to live as if you have faith, then faith begins to grow. You whistle as if you are not afraid, and that act of whistling begins to dissipate the fear.

I don't know why it took me so long to grasp this truth. I could have seen it at work in John Wesley's life because it was there plain as day. Early in his life Wesley lived a very disciplined life. He rose early in the morning for prayer. He studied the scriptures. He met with other students and together they explored the Christian faith. He gave money to the poor and visited prisoners in jail. He even traveled across the ocean to become a missionary in Georgia! In so many ways he lived an exemplary life, but, he knew something was missing. While on a ship crossing the Atlantic, there was a storm and Wesley was terrified, fearing he would die. On that ship were some Moravians, German speaking Christians, who were having a prayer meeting and were remarkably calm and at peace. Wesley knew that they had a depth of faith he did not have, but wanted intensely. He wrote in his journal, "I went to America to convert the Indians, but oh, who shall convert me?" Later, Wesley approached Peter Bohler and told him he was considering abandoning his preaching because of his weak faith. Bohler replied, "Preach faith until you have it. Then, because you have it, you will preach faith." That sounds familiar doesn't it? It sounds like "acting as if." Wesley followed Bohler's advice and he became strong in faith.

The scripture from the gospel of Mark expresses it. The father wanted his son to be cured of his illness. He wasn't sure how much he believed in Jesus, but his son had been ill since birth, and he had tried everything else he had known to try. The father heard stories of people who had been healed by Jesus. So, even with his limited faith, the father reached out to Jesus and said, "If you can do anything, have pity on us and help us." Jesus replied, "What do you mean, if you can? All things are possible to him who believes." The father said, "Lord, I believe. Help my unbelief."

That is one of the great passages in all the pages of scripture. The father did not wait until he was strong in faith. He acted on what little faith he had while praying for more. That's exactly the way it works. If you don't have faith, you act "as if." If you have only a little faith, you use what you have. It is by *acting* by faith that faith grows.

Look at the example of the disciples. When they were called into discipleship by Jesus, they didn't know who he was or where he was taking them. There must have been something attractive and magnetic about him because it was a risky thing to leave their familiar and secure patterns of living to follow him. But, don't you see, they had to follow him before they could learn who he was. First they *acted* on faith and then they came to faith.

That is something important about the life of faith that most people have missed. Faith is not primarily a feeling. It does not require emotional goose bumps. Faith is trust – a living, acting trust. You don't wait for the feeling. You act "as if," and then, in God's good time, the feeling comes. There are times in my life when I *feel* all alone. I *feel* that I have been abandoned and forsaken, and that God is nowhere to be found. I hope you have discovered, as I have, that you cannot always trust your feelings to tell you the truth. In fact, our feelings sometimes lie to us, producing fear instead of faith. Yet, it is precisely those times when we feel most devoid of faith that we need it the most.

Listen now because I'm about to say something important: at those times of need, when I *feel* that God is not present, I try to remember that faith is not a feeling, it is trust. So, no matter how I feel at a given moment, I place my trust in the promises of God: "God is our refuge and strength, a very present help in times of trouble. The eternal God is our refuge and underneath are the everlasting arms." I remember the reassuring words of Jesus, "Remember, I am with you always, even to the end of the world." I remember those promises and I trust that God is present and that He has hold of me even if my weak faith has caused me to lose my grip on Him. Even without the feelings, I *act* on faith. I act "as if" my faith is strong. And then, my faithful acting begins to erode my fear and strengthen my faith!

I have a favorite quote which I hold close when the going gets tough: "Never doubt in the darkness what God has shown you in the light." Even if you don't feel it in a given moment, you trust it. You trust those things you *know* in the deep places in your heart. You trust in those things God has shown you when your faith was strong. You build your life on that. You act "as if" those things are true, because when you are at your best, you know they are!

The principle of "acting as if" works in so many dimensions of life. Several years ago, I published a book on marriage entitled, "Marriage Is For Adults." In the book I wrote about the importance of acting lovingly even at those times when we don't feel loving. The idea is that loving actions help produce good experiences and good experiences help to produce better feelings. So, you don't wait to feel loving before you act lovingly. You act lovingly, the loving action produces a good experience, and the good experience helps you to feel more loving. It's the principle of acting "as if."

It may even work physiologically. The late Charles Allen helped me to understand it in one of his books. As a young preacher, he developed difficulty with his throat. Countless people told him that if he didn't change his way of preaching, he would lose his voice. But, no matter what he tried, nothing helped. One day a retired preacher told him, "I can tell you how to solve your problem. Just relax your hands. Relax your hands and the rest of the body will follow." Charles Allen began intentionally to relax his hands while preaching and as a result, he never again had difficulty with his throat. In telling this story, Dr. Allen concluded, "You may not think I'm much of a preacher, but I've got the most relaxed hands..." Does that have a familiar ring to it? Relax the hands and the throat will follow. Whistle a happy tune with your lips and your heart will follow. Act "as if" you have faith and faith will follow. It's all acting "as if."

Don't misunderstand. I'm not talking about pretending or being phony. Jesus warned about that. He was constantly in tension with the Scribes and Pharisees, whom he called hypocrites. He criticized them not because they failed to live up to their ideals; that describes all the best people I know. I would hate to have ideals so low that I could live up to them. No, that is not what a hypocrite is. Jesus criticized the Scribes and Pharisees for *pretending* to be something they never *intended* to be. They were intent upon appearing, not becoming.

That's not what I am talking about when I suggest acting "as if." We don't act in a certain way because that is the way we want to *appear* to others. No, we act "as if" because that is who we really want to be. Here is the essence of it: decide who you want to be; think about how that kind of person would act; begin to act in those ways; then, as you act like the person you would like to be, your actions will help to shape you into that person!

Look again at Anna's song, and let its truth find its way into your heart:

> "Make believe you're brave and the trick will take you
> far;
> You may be as brave as you make believe you are."

Acting "as if." "Lord, I believe. Help my unbelief."

Prayer: Father, there are times more numerous than we would like to admit when fear comes and shoves our faith aside. We feel alone and helpless, and we wonder if You are really there, and whether or not You really care. But we do want to live by faith. We want the warmth and security of Your near presence. So, help us day by day to act in faith. We trust Your promise that You are always with us, and that by acting in faith, we will grow in faith. Lord, we believe. Help our unbelief. Amen.

Tradition!

---

2 Thessalonians 2:15; 2 Corinthians 5:17

In the musical, "Fiddler on the Roof," the curtain opens to show us the little village of Anatevka in Russia. Perched precariously on the roof of a house is a fiddler, playing an engaging melody. The fiddler continues to play as Tevye, the central character in the musical appears. He is a husband to Golde and a father to three unmarried girls. He is a milkman who scratches out a meager living delivering milk from door to door. Gesturing toward the little man on the roof, Tevye begins to speak: "A fiddler on the roof. Sounds crazy, no? But in the little village of Anatevka, you might say every one of us is a fiddler on the roof, trying to scratch out a pleasant, simple tune without breaking his neck. It isn't easy! You may ask, 'Why do we stay up there if it's so dangerous?' We stay because Anatevka's our home. And how do we keep our balance? That I can tell you in one word: Tradition! Because of our traditions, we've kept our balance for many years. Here in Anatevka we have our traditions for everything – how to eat, how to sleep, how to work, even how to wear clothes. For instance, we always keep our heads covered, we wear these little prayer shawls – that shows our constant devotion to God. You may ask, 'How did this tradition get started?' I will tell you – I don't know! But it's a tradition! Because of our traditions, everyone here in Anatevka knows who he is and what God expects him to do. Without our traditions, our life would be as shaky as…as…a fiddler on the roof!"

think about traditions? Are they positive influences in
[...]re they negative? Do they open life up, or do they close
[...] Are they enlivening, or are they deadening? My unequivocal
[...]s – it all depends! In Tevye's village of Anatevka, their traditions
[...]ed them to endure a hard life of poverty. They helped them
[...]rvive harsh persecution from the authorities. And, as Tevye said, their
traditions helped them to know who they were and what God expected
them to do. Tradition helped them keep their balance!

At the same time, some of their traditions enslaved them. There
in Anatevka, no new ideas were encouraged and no new patterns of
behavior were allowed. Things had remained the same for generations.
They were not open to future newness. For example, marriages were
arranged by matchmakers. The matches were made and agreements
were enacted by the fathers - no romance and no falling in love.
Marriages were arranged and that's how it was done. It was a tradition!

And that is where the drama of "Fiddler on the Roof" begins: Tevye's
three daughters fantasized about meeting the man of their dreams,
falling in love, and living happily ever after. They were terrified of being
forced to marry someone they did not love. But, that is how it was done
and always had been. The first challenge to their traditions came when
Tevye promised his oldest daughter Tzeitel to Lazar Wolf, the butcher,
and they had shaken hands on it. But, in the meanwhile, she had fallen
in love and wanted to marry the man she loved. She begged her father
for permission to follow her heart.

What was Tevye to do? He was caught between his tradition and his
love for his daughter. Something had to give. In this case, his love for his
daughter won out and that part of the tradition began to change.

But everything can't be subject to change, can it? Up here on the
shaky roof of life, none of us could keep our balance if there were no
changeless, dependable dimensions to life. If everything were up for
grabs in every generation, life would be utter chaos. Unless there is
some fixed point on the compass, there is no way to know where we are
or where we are going. So, what is changeable and what is changeless?
What of our traditions are dependable and what are disposable? Those
are tough questions.

I have often said that every Christian must be a liberal conservative,
or a conservative liberal. Since we Christians are in the redemption
business, we should be about the task of redeeming those two good

words which have been so badly distorted! If you are a conservative all the time, or a liberal all the time, you will be wrong at least half of the time. For life to be well lived, there must be a balance between conserving and changing.

Clearly, there are values of the past which must be learned, valued, conserved, and lived out. There is no need to re-invent the wheel in every generation. The things we have learned at great cost from the past must be conserved. In the midst of pervasive change, there are realities which are changeless – conservative.

At the same time, we must be liberal in the sense of being open to new expressions of God's truth. We do worship a living God. He is a God of the present and the future as well as of the past. We believe in a God who has not said His last word or done His last deed. We must not be so entangled with the things God has revealed in the past that we fail to hear and respond to the truth God seeks to reveal at our time in history. We must be open to new truth – liberal.

That is why we must be liberal conservatives or conservative liberals. We must value the past and learn from it, while at the same time being open to God's new future. Both are important. Rightly understood, the best traditions are not like a prison but like a platform, giving us a firm place to stand, while we leap into the newness of God's future.

The Apostle Paul believed in conserving the best of the past, while moving out in faith toward a new future. In his letter to the Thessalonians he wrote, "Stand firm and hold fast to the traditions that you were taught by us" – conservative. At the same time, he wrote to the Corinthians, "If anyone is in Christ, there is a new creation: the old as passed away, see everything has become new!" – liberal.

So, in the gospel, there is a balance between old and new, between conserving and changing. It is never the part of wisdom simply to cling to the old because it is old. Nor is it wise to rush to the new just because it is new. What we need is some dependable standard, some way of distinguishing between that which must be conserved and that which safely can be changed or discarded.

The image Paul used earlier in his letter to the Corinthians continues to speak to me. He writes about the "treasure in earthen vessels." What he means by that is that we weak and flawed human beings have been honored by being entrusted with the message of the gospel. We are the "earthen vessels" who can tell of God's grace and power even though we are all, as one translation puts it, "cracked pots." There is that stimulating image - the treasure in earthen vessels. The eternal question is: what is the timeless treasure and what is the timely vessel in which it is placed. We have got to be clear about which is which.

That has been a problem throughout human history. Because we have not always been clear about the treasure, we have too often clung to the container as if *it* were the treasure. In Paul's first century world they wrestled with it. Some Jewish Christians insisted that circumcision, dietary laws, and Sabbath observance were all part of the treasure and were, therefore, changeless. Paul and the Gentile Christians insisted that all of that was the Jewish container and that the treasure was Christ himself. If the Jewish Christians wanted to continue all of those things as a matter of their Jewish heritage, that was fine, but they were not to confuse those things with the treasure, and try to impose them upon everyone else.

Tevye had a similar decision to make. Was marriage arranged by a matchmaker part of the changeless treasure given by God, or was it part of the cultural container and thus subject to change? The contemporary church struggles with it too. Does authentic worship require pipe organs, anthems, and traditional sermons (all in my comfort zone, I admit), or is all of that simply part of the container? Can the gospel also be celebrated by guitars, bongo drums, and PowerPoint presentations? It is okay to have preferences, but don't confuse your preferences with the treasure.

Somehow we must discover a standard by which to distinguish between that which must be conserved and that which can be changed. In other words, what is the standard by which we recognize the treasure? Listen now, because I'm about to say something important: for us, as Christians, the standard is Jesus. Jesus is the one most perfect revelation of God and God's will for His people, so we measure everything by Jesus. We walk with Jesus through the pages of the gospels. We listen to him, learn from him, and catch something of his spirit. Then we ask the question posed in the title of my last book, "Does It Look and Sound Like Jesus?" If it looks and sounds like Jesus, it is the treasure. If it doesn't measure up to that standard, it is changeable or even disposable.

It is obvious, isn't it, that traditions can be either dangerous or essential. They can be dangerous if they blind us to new truth, if they stifle growth, or if they make us satisfied with what is. At the same time, the right traditions are essential in helping us learn from the past, in giving us a perspective from which to see, and in providing a firm foundation from which to step into a new future. Again, the standard is Jesus – we measure everything by him!

I want to affirm the importance of the right traditions. As Tevye said, the right traditions help us to know who we are and what God expects us to do. They give us stability up here on the shaky roof of life. How have the Jewish people survived persecution century after century, being forced to move from place to place? Tradition – Torah, Sabbath observance, and ritual. In "Fiddler on the Roof", the entire Jewish population of Anatevka was forced to leave their home. But, we knew they would survive. We knew it, because of their tradition!

We McCormicks have family traditions. We gather on special occasions like Thanksgiving and Christmas and we go through family rituals. We eat the same foods. We join hands around the table for prayer. We have a way of giving out the gifts at Christmas. It takes hours, but it's our way of doing it. And, as we do it, memories of other Thanksgiving and Christmas celebrations come flooding in, including those with family members who have died. So, by our family ritual, the past becomes present, our relationships are strengthened, and we know who we are as McCormicks. I am sure that we would not be who we are without our traditions.

I love wedding traditions. Every time we go to a wedding, it is a special time not only for those getting married, but also for all of us who have been married for a long time. Whenever we hear those words, "… for better, for worse, for richer, for poorer, in sickness and in health," they bring back memories. We take the vows again, and our lives are enriched through tradition.

The pledge to the flag, the singing of our school's "alma mater", the bugler playing taps, or the bagpipe playing "Amazing Grace" at a graveside are all empowering traditions, helping us to know who we are, and what we are to do. How could we possibly know all of that without our traditions?

For generations, Christians have kept our balance through our sacramental traditions. The sacrament of baptism and the sacrament of Holy Communion have helped us to know who we are and what God would have us do.

Baptism is the initiatory rite by which we are incorporated into the Christian community. It means, for Christians, what circumcision has meant to Jews for centuries. I like to think of baptism as "being branded" with the brand of Christ. It means that we belong to Christ and we always will.

Holy Communion is the sacrament given to us at the Last Supper. As Jesus broke the bread and passed the cup he said, "This is my body... this is my blood. Do this as often as you will, in remembrance of me."

We often speak of Baptism and Holy Communion as symbols, as they are. A symbol is something physical that signifies something spiritual, like a flag, a wedding ring, a handshake, a hug, and a kiss. Just so, the water of Baptism and the bread and wine of Communion are symbols, and symbols are powerful expressions of meaning. But sacraments are more than symbols. Both in Baptism and in Holy Communion we remember Jesus. We remember his wise and inspiring words, his loving life, his redeeming death, his powerful resurrection, his promise to be with us always, and his assurance that he will come again and receive us to himself so that we can be with him always. And, as we remember all of that, an amazing thing happens: as we remember Jesus, the past becomes present, Christ himself joins us and gives us love and guidance and strength - everything we need to be his faithful followers. So, sacrament is more than symbol. Christ himself is present in Baptism and Holy Communion. In these two sacraments, we hold fast to the traditions we have been taught, *and* we become the new creation in Christ. We conserve and we become new. In the sacraments we know who we are and what God expects us to do. Thanks be to God!

Prayer: Loving Father, we give You thanks for the life giving traditions You have given to us. Help us to embrace them and use them to become more faithful followers of Christ. We pray in His name. Amen.

Sunrise, Sunset

Ephesians 5:15-17

"Fiddler on the Roof" is a delightful story of Tevye, a milkman, and his wife, Golde, who live with their three daughters in the little Russian town of Anatevka just after the turn of the century. They are poor, hard working peasants. Tevye talks regularly with God about his problems, about his longing to be rich, with time to read the holy book, and to sit hour by hour with the rabbis to discuss their faith. Life in Anatevka is hard, but life is sustained by faith and by their traditions, which define each person's role and lay out the expectations of the community. For generations they have lived and died according to their traditions. We talked about that in the previous chapter.

The oldest daughter of Tevye and Golde is Tzeitel. Tradition insists that she must be the first to marry and that her marriage must be arranged by a matchmaker. But, in violation of the tradition, Tzeitel falls in love with Motel, a poor tailor who does not even own his own sewing machine! Although Tzeitel has been promised to another, and Tevye and the prospective groom had shaken hands on it, Tzeitel begs and pleads for permission to marry Motel. Finally Tevye relents and gives his permission and his blessing for Tzeitel and Motel to marry. After all, he really does love his family and he wants his daughters to be happy.

One of the most moving scenes in the musical is the wedding. The music is lush and memorable. Tzeitel and Motel stand beneath the traditional Jewish wedding canopy facing the rabbi. Tevye and Golde look lovingly at these two young people about to be married and begin to think back over the years leading to this moment. The music begins…

"Is this the little girl I carried, is this the little boy at play?
I don't remember growing older, when did they?
When did she get to be a beauty, when did he grow to be so tall?
Wasn't it yesterday when they were small?
Sunrise, sunset, sunrise, sunset, swiftly flow the days,
Seedlings turn overnight to sunflowers, blossoming even as we gaze.
Sunrise, sunset, sunrise, sunset, swiftly fly the years,
One season following another, laden with happiness and tears."

I seldom hear or read those words without them bringing a tear to my eyes, because what they state so beautifully is true – the years do flow so swiftly. When we are young time seems to move more slowly. Christmas never seems to come. The birthday which qualifies us for our first driver's license seems an eternity away. But, as we grow older, time begins to pick up speed until the days and the years fairly fly away.

I identify with the feelings of Tevye and Golde, questioning, "Where have the years gone?" Our two children are adults now, with children of their own. But it seems that only a few weeks ago I was putting training wheels on Mark's first bicycle, and only a few days ago coaching his Little League baseball team. It seems that just recently I was teaching Lynne how to dance, with her little feet placed on top of mine as we moved to the music. It's true – swiftly flow the days and years, much more swiftly than most of us would like. And, once they are gone, there is no bringing them back or living them over. What is done is done, for good or for ill.

That is why Paul, in his letter to the Ephesians, gave this word of caution, "Be careful about the life you lead: act like sensible people (not like those who do not know the meaning and purpose of life) make the very best use of your time." As we think about "Sunrise, Sunset," consider what it means to make the best use of time in our relationships, especially in family relationships.

First, make time for growing. Seedlings turning overnight into sunflowers is good imagery because it gives us a picture of growth, and growth is a central purpose of life for every one of us. We don't come into life as complete human beings. We are born as little packages of potential, and our task is to develop that potential and become all that we are capable of becoming.

I believe that God, in His wisdom, created us and placed us in families, because it is in families that we have the best chance of growing in the right ways. As we help one another grow, it is important to realize that every human being is unique and special. God does not create "cookie cutter" people. There are no two of us alike; instead, each of us is a unique and unrepeatable miracle of God's creative power. Each of us has his or her own gifts, interests, personalities and potentialities. Since each of us is "different," nothing good ever comes from trying to compare one person with another. And, certainly it is not good to devalue a person because he or she is "different". We are *all* different. What is asked of us is to look carefully and gently at those we love – to look for unique, buried gifts, and to tenderly coax them out of hiding. We are to encourage those gifts into blossoming growth, "seedlings into sunflowers."

The best atmosphere for growth is one in which every person knows that he or she is loved, valued, and cared about, and that none of that is conditional. It doesn't depend upon our performance. We simply know, deep down, that we are loved, *period*. We may be criticized, put down, and ridiculed everywhere else, but at home we know that we are loved *no matter what!* Wherever that atmosphere exists, it is beautiful.

While we are talking about growth, let us note that there is growing to be done at every stage of life. We never complete the process. We never graduate. We never arrive. There will never come a time when we can say, "I've learned all I need to know. I've grown as much as I need to grow. I've become all I need to become." No, once we stop growing we begin to die, so growth must be a continuing goal of retired grandparents as well as of pre-schoolers. The good news is that every stage of life has its own beauty and meaning. So, whatever your stage of life, take the time to enjoy it because it will be over before you know it.

I am sure you will confess with me the difficulty of living fully in each given moment. The temptation is either to relive or regret the past or to anticipate the future, and thus allow the present moment to slip from our grasp. We look forward to the time when infants will sleep through the night, to the time when they begin to walk and talk, to the time when they are potty trained, to the time when they start to school, to the time when they are old enough to leave with a sitter, to the time when they can drive, to the time when they are in college, to the time when they are married, and on and on it goes. The danger is that, in anticipating the next stage of growth, we fail to embrace the wonder of the present moment. Each moment has a beauty of its own, when we can see it.

How many of us would like to go back and re-live some of those moments we failed to see, touch, and experience? Time flies so quickly. Do you sense the poignancy of the words, "I don't remember growing older. When did they?" But it is too late to go back. All we can do is to make sure we don't miss the next moment.

Let me make one more observation about making time for growing. One reason children are given parents is that they don't come into the world fully grown. There is much learning to be done and parents are the primary teachers, at least initially. The best learning experiences begin with discipline and end with freedom. Too many parents try to start with freedom and impose discipline later, but that doesn't work. When we are wise, we begin with a structured life, instruction, guidance, and "do's" and "don'ts." The child has the security of knowing that someone who loves him and has had some experience in living is there and available. There is security in knowing what the limits are and what the expectations are. Healthy growth can take place in such an environment.

The tricky part is that, as growth takes place, more and more freedom is granted. The fences are gradually moved out and the maturing youth makes more and more decisions on his own until he is able to take responsibility for his own decisions as an adult. The wise parent knows how quickly to grant freedom and when to let go and to begin relating to children as adults. Tevye and Golde struggled with it, but finally they set their children free and loved them as adults.

It is clear that growth toward maturity is a major goal of life, and the family is where that happens best. Don't miss the beauty of any stage of growth, and don't miss the opportunity of any moment. As Paul said, "Make the very best use of your time." Make time for growth.

Second, make time for loving. As the song says, a mixture of happiness and tears is normal in life, and the tears are bearable and the happiness is magnified when those experiences are shared with those we love.

In "Fiddler on the Roof" there are some disappointments and disagreements in Tevye's household, but it is abundantly clear that their love for one another permeates it all. When love is there and family members know it, that provides an atmosphere in which hurts can be healed, mistakes forgiven, and failures overcome.

I remember visiting a friend of mine in the hospital. He had been critically ill but was improving, and he wanted to talk about the importance of loving relationships. He commented on the all too prevalent chase after money, position, status, and pleasure. "But," he said from his hospital bed, "none of that can compare with loving and being loved." He continued, "Sometimes it takes a crisis to make you see what is really important in life, and then it's often too late. But nothing in life can compare with loving the members of your family and being loved by them."

I wholeheartedly agree! There are a great many things in life that I care about, but my family is in a league by itself. I don't have words large enough to describe it, but there are times when I feel like weeping for the sheer joy of loving and being loved by my family!

That is an experience no one wants to miss. Don't let it be covered over by a thousand and one busy involvements. Don't let past hurts keep you from it. Make time for listening to one another, and make time for doing things together. Make it a priority.

A young service man had enough close calls to make him do some heavy thinking about life and its meaning. He thought about the tendency for our homes to be "filling stations", with members busily coming and going, eating, sleeping, and doing laundry, but seldom taking the time to really *know* one another or to touch one another beneath the surface. From overseas, this service man wrote a letter to his parents, saying, "You know, I have a feeling that I am coming home all right. What I want to say is – when I do get home, I hope that, when we have finished dinner at night, and we're all there at the table, we will just stay there and look at one another, and realize for just a little while nothing else but the fact that we are there together and that we love each other. That's all I want." There is nothing more important. Make time for loving.

In addition to making time for growing and for loving, life will not be complete unless we also make time for worshipping. Paul wrote, "Be careful about the life you lead: act like sensible people (not like those who do not know the meaning and purpose of life)."

People of faith have always understood that the meaning and purpose of life is all tied up with a relationship with God, and if you miss that, you miss life at its best. No one ever said it better than Augustine, "Thou hast made us for Thyself, O God, and our hearts are restless 'til they find their rest in Thee."

From a faith perspective, that is what life is all about, and you would think that Christian families would see to it that all those they care about know that and are committed to that. There is nothing in life as essential as a relationship with the God who is the creator and sustainer of all of life.

As a Pastor, there are few things as disappointing as the laxity of parents in giving sound teaching and example to their children. I see parents taking great care to insure that their children have nice homes, lovely clothes, excellent schools, enjoyable activities, and the best in health care. We don't want our children to miss any good thing in life – we want that because we love them. How then can we be so casual about their relationship with God? If they don't have God, they don't have the best – don't you know that? No one has a better opportunity to put those you love into contact with God than you do. Don't pass that off to the pastor, the Sunday school teacher, or the friend down the block. You parents, you grand-parents, you brothers and sisters, it's your job. I want to be sure that my children and my grandchildren become God's children in faith, not in spite of me, but because of me. There is nothing I have to do that is more important!

Of course, it is clear to me that I cannot give someone else a faith that I do not have, so I must first get my own house in order. If I want others to become persons of faith, I must first insure that *I* am a person of faith.

During my growing up years, I knew that my parents were God's people. It was obvious. Our family was centered in God, and faith in God was as much a part of the atmosphere around me as the air I breathed. I never heard the question, "Shall we go to worship today?" If it was Sunday, we went. We never started a meal without thanking God. Among my earliest memories is waking up in the morning and going into my parents' bedroom to find my mother sitting there in the sunshine near a window through which she could see the birds and her flowers, and reading her Bible. Every morning! How is that for a legacy! As a result, very early in my life I came to know who I am as God's child and I came to know what life is all about as God's creation. All of that is just who we were as a family. God was real and God was essential. And my life was shaped in profoundly important ways because we made time for worship.

Sadly, as a Pastor, I have seen what often happens in families where God is neither real nor important. Other priorities come to the fore, God gets shoved to the bottom of the list, and life is taken for granted. Great care is taken to insure that children are well fed, well housed, well educated, and well entertained, but all too often parents do not take equal care to insure that they are well nurtured in faith. But when a crisis comes, and – I've see it so many times – the parents want the church to provide instant values, instant perspective, and instant faith. Of course, we do what we can, but I can't help thinking about the wasted opportunities when faith did not seem so important.

I remember a young man who was dying. His father was sitting anxiously by his bed. The boy said to his father, "You have given me everything money can buy – education, recreation, things. But dad, you never told me about God, and I am dying, and I'm afraid."

Like all good parents, I want my children and grandchildren to have all the good things money can buy. But I want even more for them to have those essential things that money cannot buy, and if they miss out on God, they have missed the best in life. So, as those who know the meaning and purpose of life, make time for worship. Make the very best use of your time.

The good news is that it's never too late. We can never go back and re-live the past, but it is never too late to start over in a new direction, so that, from now on, we make time for growing, for loving, and for worshipping. We are not alone, you know. God is with us, and God wants to bless our families through us. He wants to give every one of His children the very best in life. It is because God loves us so much that He gives us families to love us too!

Listen to Paul again, "Be careful about the life you lead: act like sensible people (not like those who do not know the meaning and purpose of life); make the very best use of your time."

Prayer: Father, we are grateful for loving relationships with You, our friends, and our families. Help us to make the most of the opportunities which are ours. Let us not miss any chance for growing, loving, and worshipping. Accept our thanks now for those we love and for those who love us. In Jesus' name we pray. Amen.

Do You Love Me?

John 21:15-19

In "Fiddler on the Roof," life in the little Russian village of Anatevka is hard. People struggle to keep their balance and to survive from one day to the next. It isn't easy! With all the hardships of life, Tevye says that it is as difficult to keep your balance as it is for a fiddler to stand on a steep roof top, playing his fiddle, without falling off.

In the scene we will look at in this chapter, a series of events have occurred which make life in Anatevka even more difficult. Tevye's daughters were getting married, and in violation of their tradition, the marriages were not arranged by a matchmaker. They chose their mates, young men with whom they had fallen in love! Russian soldiers were making raids on the Jewish settlement. People were frightened of the future and some were leaving. If all of that were not enough, Tevye's horse had become lame and Tevye himself was having to pull his milk cart through town to make deliveries.

When troubles multiply, you have to get down to basics. You begin to ask some serious questions, wanting to know what is dependable and what you can count on. Tevye begins to think about his marriage to Golde. The daughters had married for love, but Tevye and Golde had their marriage arranged by a matchmaker. They had not even met before the day of their wedding. Their parents had told them that they would learn to love each other. They had been married for twenty-five years and Tevye wanted to know if the promise had been fulfilled. Tevye goes into their house and asks his wife a question. He asks, "Golde, do you love me?"

There is a down-to-earth truthfulness in the exchange that followed. When Tevye raised the question of love, Golde was surprised. Probably they had not spoken of such things before. She became embarrassed by the question and then evasive: "With our daughters getting married and this trouble in the town, you're upset, you're worn out, go inside, go lie down. Maybe it's indigestion!" Tevye was persistent, so Golde gave her answer. I think it was right on target. She expressed a truth that is basic and profound. She talked about the things she had been *doing* for twenty-five years of marriage – concrete and tangible expressions of her love. For twenty-five years she had washed his clothes, cooked his meals, cleaned the house, given him children, and milked the cow. She concluded, "For twenty-five years I've lived with him, fought with him, starved with him. For twenty-five years my bed is his; if that's not love, what is?"

Instinctively Golde understood a truth which escapes many of us. She knew that in addition to all the words about love and all the feelings of love, love basically is *something you do!* Of course, it would have been better if Tevye and Golde had expressed their love in ways in addition to earning a living, cleaning the house, and milking the cow. Such everyday tasks are an important part of our expression of love, but it would have been nice to share an occasional kiss or embrace – something personal and something more obviously romantic.

The healthiest families are those in which such demonstrations of affection are open and obvious. Children learn how to relate by watching how mom and dad relate. I often see people in counseling who find it difficult to express affection because they seldom saw it in their home and they were seldom given affection by their parents. It is difficult to give what you have not received.

The same holds true between friends as well. A warm handclasp or embrace can be a meaningful and personal way of expressing our affection, and everyone needs that. Someone has suggested that four hugs is the minimum adult daily requirement. The point is that words are not enough. Feelings are not enough. Love is not love until you show it in some way. Don't ever forget that: whatever else it may be, love is something you do.

That is something I stress in talking with couples about to be married. When a couple is in love and planning to be married, the loving feelings are beautiful. In the euphoria of such feelings it is easy to take the vows of marriage. The problem is that feelings are undependable and uncontrollable. Unfortunately, you can't feel good and loving toward anyone all of the time. There are times in every marriage when we don't like each other very much. That is normal. The thing I try to stress is that you don't have to wait until you *feel* loving to *act* lovingly, because, after all, love is something you do. We can't control our feelings, but as mature human beings we can control our actions. We can decide to act lovingly even when we don't feel loving. That loving action will create a good experience, and the good experience will help us to feel loving again. That is how loving feelings can be renewed again and again – not waiting for feelings, but deciding to act lovingly. Love that has grown up to maturity is understood as something you do.

I remember hearing about a young man with a well developed case of "puppy love." Romantic feelings seemed to ooze from every pore of his body. He sat down to write a note to his sweetheart. As he wrote, no expression of love was too strong and no adjective was too intense. He wrote, "Darling, I love you. My love is like a red, red rose that blooms for you alone. It is like the nectar of the gods. It is my soul's delight. Because of it, I would travel to the ends of the earth for you. I would dare the greatest dangers. I would fight my way to your side though giants should oppose me. Through storm and fire I would persevere to reach you. Accept this as the expression of my undying love. Yours forever, John. P.S. I will be over to see you on Tuesday if it doesn't rain."

The first time I heard that story, I thought immediately of the words of an anonymous sage who said, "What you do speaks so loudly I can't hear a word you're saying." That is true, isn't it? All of that young man's pretty, flowery words were cancelled out by his refusal to put them into action.

I hope you hear what I am saying: love is more than sentimental feelings. Love is more than flowery rhetoric. Love in the basic, Christian sense of the word is something you do.

Jesus talked a great deal about love. He felt it was so important that, after the resurrection, he spent his last moments with Simon Peter talking about it. Three times he asked Peter, "Do you love me?" Three times Peter answered in the affirmative. Many Bible scholars believe that

Jesus was giving Peter three opportunities to affirm his love as a way of atoning for the three times he had denied Jesus. Listen now: each time Peter affirmed his love, Jesus asked him to *do something* as an expression of his love. Jesus asked Peter to feed his sheep.

What that event says to us is that, while loving feelings are good, while verbal expressions of love are necessary, the fact is that the authenticity of love is demonstrated by what we do. "Do you love me?" asked Jesus. "If you do, then feed my sheep."

Anyone can say flowery things when we are caught up in the emotion of a moment. The test comes when we are called to move from rhetoric to action. Do you remember when, at the Last Supper, Peter said that even if everyone else ran away and forsook Jesus, he would never betray him. In the sentiment of that moment, I am sure that Peter was sincere, but when the test came, and Peter was required to give substance to his words, he was afraid, and he denied Jesus three times. At that time in his life his love consisted mostly of sentiment – warm feelings – but not much backbone and follow through. It was later, after the resurrection, that his love grew up to maturity and he was ready to act lovingly as well as feel loving.

Let me say it again – this truth affirmed both by the exchange between Jesus and Peter and by the conversation between Tevye and Golde – listen carefully because this is the heart of it: love is not love until you show it in some way. Love is something you *do.*

Let me hasten to add: that doesn't mean that words are not important – they are! Love is something you do – that's true. But love is also something you need to say. That's true too. For too long we have tried to make words and actions enemies of one another, as if they are antithetical, but they are not. It is not a matter of loving actions *or* loving words. It is a matter of *both/and.*

When Jesus walked with Simon Peter, he emphasized the importance of following through on his love – expressing his love by feeding Jesus' sheep. But, apparently, it was also important to Jesus to hear the words as well. He kept asking the question, "Do you love me?" because he wanted to hear Peter say it!

In our culture, we downplay too much the importance of words. I believe that there is power in words – tremendous power – especially when there is a consistency between what we say and what we do. Words are only empty and meaningless when they are not reinforced by our deeds. I believe it is essential to express our love by doing loving things, and when those loving actions are followed by loving words, those words come to us like rain in a parched desert. We all need to hear the words, "I love you."

It's too bad, isn't it, that so many of us have difficulty saying that? Christopher Morley once wrote, "If the population was warned that they had five minutes until sudden death, the telephone lines would be jammed with people telling other people that they love them." But, because we don't sense imminent death, too often we fail to express our love.

I remember one of Ann Landers' columns in which she made a plea for more freedom in expressing love for one another. A husband responded that he had made it clear to his wife when they married that he loved her. He also planned to let her know immediately if there was ever a change in his feelings. So, in the meanwhile, he saw no need to speak of love. Isn't that sad?

I am not altogether sure why so many are reluctant to speak of love. Perhaps we fear rejection and our love will not be returned. Perhaps we fear embarrassment; we don't want to look foolish. Perhaps we fear that to express our feelings makes us vulnerable and open to hurt. We seem to sense that it is risky to express our feelings and that is true. We can be hurt by loving and by expressing our love. But that is not the greatest risk. The greatest risk of all is to try to protect ourselves by not expressing love, because that cuts us off from loving relationship, and without loving relationships we die. It is risky to put love into words, but it is a risk worth taking because it moves us toward life at its best.

I remember some words from a poem my father used to quote. It's not great poetry, but there is a recurring refrain that has never left my mind: "If you love him let him know it. If you love him why not show it, for he cannot read his tombstone when he's dead." I'm not sure about not being able to read our tombstones, but the main part of the statement is utterly true. Why wait until someone dies to say nice things about them or to them? Why be so reluctant to express our love here and now, and in unmistakable ways? Let's decide to take that risk because it is worth it.

I love the dialogue between Tevye and Golde. Golde was right on target in pointing to all of the loving things she had done in their twenty-five years of marriage. It is absolutely true that love is something you do.

But Tevye still wanted to hear the words. He sensed, correctly, that love is *also* something you say. At the conclusion of their song, after Golde says, "If that's not love, what is?" Tevye says, "Then you love me?" She replies, "I suppose I do." Tevye smiles and says, "And I suppose I love you too." Then they sing together, "It doesn't change a thing, but even so, after twenty-five years, it's nice to know."

Yes, it is nice to know. It's nice to experience loving actions, but it's also nice to hear loving words. I love the dialogue between Tevye and Golde and the song they sing together. It's all delightful, and most of what they say is right on target, but in one instance they missed the target by a mile. When they say is doesn't change a thing to say and hear the words, they are wrong. They just are! I believe that a relationship takes on a new and deeper meaning when we are able to *say* "I love you," as well as *act out* "I love you." Everyone needs to hear words of love, and more than we know, everyone needs the experience of saying them.

Let me bring it together and underline it like this: in his little book, "The Secret of Staying in Love," Father John Powell relates this story. There were two Jesuit priests who, for many years, had experienced a rich and satisfying friendship. The two had trudged together through long seminary training and had stayed in touch for a great many years. When one of them had a special need for time, a listening ear, or whatever, the other had always been there. Then tragedy struck. One of the priests was hit by a car and killed right in front of the residence where the two men lived with their community. When the second priest learned that his dear friend of so many years lay dead on the street, he went running out through the cordon of onlookers and police and knelt at his side. He gently cradled the dead man's head on his arm and in the presence of all those gaping people, he blurted out, "Don't die! You can't die! I never told you that I love you!"

Do you hear what God has to say to us? Love is something you do. That is important to understand. But love is also something you say. That is important too.

Prayer: Father, through Your Son, Jesus, You have taught us so much. Teach us now about love. Teach us how to do it, and teach us how to say it. We sense that so much depends upon that. Father, help us to love as we have been loved by You. In Jesus' name we pray. Amen.

If I Were a Rich Man

Philippians 4:10-13

Of all the characters in "Fiddler on the Roof," my favorite is Tevye. His foibles and fantasies seem so much like my own that I can identify with him. There he is, trying to scratch out a meager living in the little village of Anatevka and having a difficult time of it. As the story unfolds, it seems that "Murphy's Law" was written just for Tevye: "When it seems that things cannot possibly get any worse, they usually do." Tevye was already in poverty and struggling when his horse goes lame, giving him all the more work to do. Then, one by one, his daughters want to marry. Who? Not wealthy, established men, but young boys ever poorer than Tevye! It is not surprising then, that in the midst of such financial difficulty, Tevye's favorite fantasy is to be a rich man. Listen...

> "If I were a rich man, ya ha deedle deedle bubba
> bubba deedle deedle dum,
> All day long I'd biddy biddy bum, if I were a wealthy
> man.
> I wouldn't have to work hard, ya ha deedle deedle
> bubba bubba deedle deedle dum
> If I were a biddy biddy rich, yidle-diddle-didle-didle
> man."

After several verses spelling out how nice it would be to be rich, he concludes,

"Lord who made the lion and the lamb, you decreed I should be what I am,
Would it spoil some vast eternal plan if I were a wealthy man?"

That is a humorous, enjoyable song and we enjoy listening to it, but if we take it seriously there is a tragic side to it. Tevye is wasting his time and energy fantasizing about a life which can never be his. Instead of living in a dream world, how much better would it be to invest his energy in being who he is and in squeezing every ounce of living out of the reality of his life.

I don't want to be too hard on Tevye because he is a lovable character whose heart is generally in the right place. I can identify with him. From time to time we all get caught up in fantasies and go running off in pursuit of illusions. I believe, however, that the Apostle Paul is a better model for us. In his letter to the Philippians, Paul is thanking them for the gift of money they have sent him. He reminds them, though, that he had not complained even when he was in need. After all, he had experienced so many difficult circumstances in his life. He had experienced plenty and he had experienced hunger, and he wrote, "I have learned, in whatever state I am, to be content."

Of course, for Paul and all of us, it is better to be well fed than to be hungry. That is just rational, and Paul was always in touch with reality. It was better to be out of prison than in. It was better to be in good health than to be ill. It was better to be well received than to be rejected. All of that is true. But Paul insisted that the quality of his life was not dependent upon the circumstances in which he found himself. He had taken hold of a reality which enabled him to live and to be content whatever his circumstances. He did not have to spend his time and energy saying, "If only this could happen; if only I could be like that; if only I had this." No, instead he put forth this remarkable witness, "I have learned, in whatever state I am, to be content."

That is a lesson Tevye would do well to learn. It's a lesson we all should learn. So, let me say three things to all of us.

First, if you want to be content, concentrate on being who you are where you are. Many of the frustrations and disappointments of life come when we try to be like someone else, when we try to live someone else's dream for us, or when we fantasize about being in circumstances other than the ones we are in. It is difficult enough to be ourselves successfully; it's impossible to be someone else.

Have you ever thought about how insulting it is to God for us to deny who we are while longing to be someone else, somewhere else? Listen, God did not make a mistake when He created you. You are the intentional result of God's creation. No one else in the world is exactly like you. No one else can be who you are or do what you can do. You are unique. One of a kind. Since you are who you are (and that is good!), and since you can't be anyone else, success and contentment in life involves discovering who you are. It involves knowing what gifts you have, developing those gifts, and then using those gifts to the best of your ability.

Many people waste time worrying about what they don't have and can't do instead of using what they have and doing what they can. There is a poem that says it:

> "It's not what you'd do with a million, if riches should
> be your lot;
> But what are you doing today with the dollar and a
> quarter you've got?"

That is the question!

There is an old story about a couple who traveled around the world in search of wealth. Finally, after exhausting all their resources, they returned home, tired, disillusioned, and old. They returned to the starting point of their journey only to discover a vast reservoir of oil right under their doorstep, but by then they had so little time left to enjoy it.

Many people look for happiness and fulfillment everywhere except where they are, in everything except what they are already doing, and in all circumstances except those they are in. It is so tempting to look everywhere except right under our noses!

It was not possible for Tevye to be a rich man in that country at that time in history. To continue dreaming about it was escapist, a fantasy, and an illusion. Perhaps it helped him to keep his sanity, and I can understand the temptation, but I wonder if there is really any long term comfort in a lie? There was so much in Tevye's life that was worth celebrating: his love for his family and theirs for him; the respect and good will of his friends; the strength which comes from hard work and integrity; and finally, the deep religious faith which gave stability and meaning to his life. Even without being rich, Tevye could rely upon those things.

Don't misunderstand what I am saying. I don't mean to imply that we are not to have dreams. Dreams are essential. I don't want to leave the impression that we can never be more than we are at this moment. Instead, I want to make a distinction between a dream and an illusion, between a possibility and a fantasy. Also, I want to make a distinction between our attempting to become all that we can be and attempting to become something that only someone else can be.

The point is that you don't have to be like anyone else. Contentment comes from developing your gifts, not someone else's gifts; from pursuing your dreams, not someone else's dreams; from living your life, not someone else's life. You don't have to be like anyone else. You don't have to be in any different situation in order to be happy and fulfilled. You *do* have to be you, the real you, the best you. So, take permission to do that. Get all the mileage you can out of that. Learn to be content with that. As Paul said, "I have learned in whatever state I am, to be content."

The second point I want to make is that if you want to be content, reach *inside* yourself and not *outside* yourself. In the final analysis, happiness is not to be found in a certain set of circumstances, but in a certain attitude of the spirit brought to all circumstances. Tevye did not have to be rich in order to be happy. He simply had to be the best of all possible Tevyes. It is clear that circumstances do not produce happiness. I know people who go from place to place looking for the circumstances that will make them happy. The problem is that they must take themselves with them wherever they go. The one common denominator is *them!*

A person who has no strong center of being, even if he is placed in the most idyllic circumstances, will not be happy. At the same time, a person who knows who he is and is happy with who he is, even if he is in a difficult environment, will cope with it and forge a fulfilling life out of it. We do not have to be victims of our circumstances. Our lives do not have to be shaped by the atmosphere around us. Instead, we take our atmosphere with us wherever we go. We can be inner-directed rather than outer-directed persons. By God's grace, we can rise above our circumstances.

Two boys were standing in the lunch line at school. Another boy rudely pushed his way into line in front of them. Many people would have responded in kind, taking their cue from his actions, shoving back and saying some appropriate angry words. However, one of the boys was remarkably even-tempered and overlooked the incident completely. Later, his friend said to him, "Why were you so tolerant of that creep? You should have let him have it!" The boy replied, "But that's not who I am. Why should I let him decide what kind of person I am going to be?" Why indeed! That young man refused to be a victim of his surroundings. He carried his own atmosphere with him.

Another example: there was a little girl living in a run-down section of town who found a single roller skate in the alley. She could have felt sorry for herself because she didn't find two skates, but that was not the kind of person she had decided to be. She thought to herself, "Two skates are better than one, but one skate is better than none at all. So, here goes the best time any little girl ever had with one skate!"

We would do well to learn from her. Happiness and contentment are not dependent upon circumstances. They come from within. It's not what we find *out there*. It's something we *bring* to whatever we find out there. That is what Paul was saying: "I know how to be abased and I know how to abound. I have learned, in whatever state I am, to be content."

One more thing: we have been talking about reaching inside yourself and developing a center of meaning and strength inside yourself so that you are not at the mercy of the circumstances around you. The final thing I want to emphasize in this chapter is that that center of meaning and strength becomes possible when you reach inside and meet God there in your depths. It is in relationship with God that the negatives of your life become manageable and the positives of your life are enlarged and enhanced. That is how Paul did it. His statement to the Philippians did not conclude with the boast, "I have learned, in whatever state I am, to be content." Left to our own resources that is never possible. If we are totally on our own, before very long we will be caught up in and swept along with whatever negative currents are raging in our surroundings. Paul never said that he could do it by himself. He did not say, "I can do all things!" What he said was, "I can do all things through Him who strengthens me." That is how Paul did it. His all-weather, all-circumstances contentment was made possible by God!

I am inclined to say to God, "But, I'm weak. I have limitations. I am sinful. I have made so many mistakes!" But God will answer, "That is true. That is all true. But that is not *all* that is true. You may be weak and limited and sinful, but that is not all you are. Follow me and I will show you what you can be. I will make you what you can be, and I will make life good for you. That's a promise!"

Can you hear the good news in that? You don't have to be someone you are not and somewhere you are not. It is okay to be you, right where you are. "Tevye, you don't have to be rich. Stop worrying about what isn't. Celebrate what is! Your family loves you. Your friends respect and like you, and God is for you. Don't long to be someone you are not. Be the best Tevye you can be!" That is a good word for Tevye, and it is a good word for us.

Years ago, William James, the father of American psychology said that no one has ever used more than a small fraction of what he potentially is. The world is filled with unused, buried talent - because it has never been called out. I think that is at least part of what the Christian faith is about. Jesus comes to us and calls for the best within us. He says to us exactly what he said to men by the Sea of Galilee centuries ago, "Come, follow me." And in his company, we receive all we need to be ourselves, our best selves, and then to move from that strong center of ourselves to interact lovingly and helpfully with the world around us. Because of that, we are able to shape our environment for good rather than to be shaped by it.

In an art gallery in Athens, there is a statue of Apollo. It's a magnificent figure of physical perfection. Observers say it is interesting to watch people as they pass by that statue. They are not aware of what they are doing, but they hold their heads more erectly, the shoulders a bit more squarely, and their steps are made a bit more firmly. It isn't a conscious thing, but seeing that statue, people are drawn to it and are influenced by it. Seeing its perfection, they want to be like it.

That is what happens to us in the presence of Jesus. We see his authentic humanness and we want to be more human too. In his presence we catch a glimpse of what we can be, and in his strength we begin the journey of becoming all that we can be. Don't you see, that is where life is to be found...not in being someone else or being in other circumstances, but in being all that we can be right where we are. "I have learned," said Paul, "that, in whatever state I am, to be content. I can do all things through Him who strengthens me."

Prayer: Father, forgive us for wasting our time worrying about what we don't have and what we can't do. Give us an appreciation and love for ourselves as You have created us. Inspire us to give ourselves to You in the faith that what we are and what we can become by Your grace is good enough. Make us content. Make us blessed. And make us a blessing to others. We pray in the name of Jesus, who calls us to fulfillment by calling us to follow him. Amen.

Miracle of Miracles

James 1:16-17a

"Fiddler on the Roof" is a delightful musical with many engaging scenes. Every time I see it, it captures me again and I come away singing and humming all the memorable tunes. One of my favorite scenes is when Tzeitel, Tevye's oldest daughter, and Motel, the poor tailor whom she loves, finally conjure up the courage to ask Tevye for permission to marry. That was a terrifying experience! In fact, Motel compares it to the experience of Daniel in the lion's den!

The problems were many. Tradition insisted that all marriages be arranged by a matchmaker - and a very good match had already been arranged. Tzeitel was to marry Lazar Wolf, the butcher, who was a wealthy and established man. Motel was a tailor so poor that he didn't even own his own sewing machine. But Tzeitel and Motel were in love and that love gave them the courage to go to Tevye to ask his permission for them to marry. At first he refused. It was out of the question! But, with remarkable persistence and boldness they pressed their point. You could see Tevye as he struggled with it, pulled in one direction by tradition, and pulled in another by his love for his daughter. Although he was often loud, blustery, and stubborn, Tevye was really a loving, caring father at heart and so he finally gave in and granted permission for them to marry.

At first Tzeitel and Motel were surprised. The news was almost too good to be true. They were going to be married! When that truth sank in, they began to celebrate. They grinned from ear to ear. They danced all over the stage. And Motel began to sing...

> "Wonder of wonders, miracle of miracles, God took a
> Daniel once again,
> Stood by his side and, miracle of miracles, walked him
> through the lion's den!"

What a great song! The thing that impresses me most about that song is that in the presence of their good fortune, Tzeitel and Motel did not credit their cleverness, their courage, or even Tevye's loving openness. They looked at this good thing that had happened and saw in it the hand of God! That impresses me.

The reason that impresses me is because that kind of vision is so rare. The ability to look at the everyday events of life and see the divine dimension in them is not an ability everyone possesses. It requires looking at life through the eyes of faith, and when a person begins to see in that way, everything is changed. The world becomes a much larger world. We begin to see goodness and beauty and meaning that we never noticed before. Everywhere we look, we see the hand of God at work, and we begin to celebrate the wonder and miracle of life!

James had that kind of eyesight. Everywhere he looked, he saw God, and so he wrote, "Every good gift, every perfect gift is from above." Those good gifts may be conveyed in a variety of ways. They may pass through the hands of many people. But trace them all back to their source and you will discover a loving heavenly Father at work.

I love the words of Maltbie Babcock, "Back of the loaf is the snowy flour, and back of the flour, the mill, and back of the mill is the wheat and the shower and the sun and the Father's will."

That is one of the differences between people of faith and other people. People of faith don't necessarily receive more gifts from God than other people. As Jesus said, "God makes his sun shine on the evil and on the good, and sends his rain on the just and on the unjust." In whatever ways the good things of life come to us, people of faith are able to recognize them as the gifts of God. We know how to name them and who to thank for them. Further, their meaning is magnified because they cause us to celebrate that a loving and generous God is at work in our lives.

That is what James was saying, "Every good gift, and every perfect gift is from above." Once we see that and begin to celebrate that life takes on new meaning. We discover that, at every moment, we are surrounded by wonders and miracles we never saw before.

Of course, it's impossible to do justice to any listing of daily miracles for which we should be thankful. There are so many of them that to name them all would be a task too large for a lifetime, to say nothing about the brevity of one chapter in a book. But I would like to talk about three of the most important ones – the first is the miracle at the heart of the Christian gospel, and the second and third miracles are those Motel sings about in his song.

The first miracle is the miracle of God's love that comes to us through Jesus, the Christ. I have been trying to wrap my mind and heart around it all my life, but I am still amazed by the fact that God knows me as I am – not as I pretend to be, or as I would like to be – and He loves me anyway! I tell you, that's a miracle! I don't know about you, but I have difficulty loving myself, especially when my pretenses begin to crumble, my rationalizations begin to fade, and I am forced to see myself as I really am. God sees all of that and loves me still. That is why we sing about "Amazing Grace." It is amazing indeed – love that keeps on loving no matter what!

But that is what the good news is all about. The gospel declares that God does not wait for us to become worthy before He begins to love us. He doesn't set up a lot of religious hoops for us to jump through before He begins to care about us. He doesn't insist that we become good or moral as a pre-requisite for His loving. No, the good news is that "while we were still sinners, Christ died for us."

It is surely good that is true, because when I need God's love the most is when I deserve it the least. The wonder is that God's love is given to us in such an unworthy and utterly needy condition. The miracle is what begins to happen in the life of a person who is touched by that unconditional love, embraces it, and begins to live in the strength and security of it.

Carl Mays tells about it happening in a young man named Billy:

> "God created Billy and said, 'It is good.' Then Billy
>   defected – he sinned.
> Billy fell short of his potential. Billy's sin hid him from
>   himself;
> He could not find himself; he could not find God.
> Billy did not realize that he was made in the image of
>   God.
> 'Where am I?' he cried. 'Who am I?'
> Billy tried to find himself. But the dry look didn't work;
>   not even a new sex-appeal toothpaste or promising
>   mouthwash or dependable deodorant could show
>   him himself or locate God for him.
> Enter Jesus Christ! Billy stepped out on personal faith,
>   responded, and believed.
> Billy caught a glimpse of himself and God. Billy liked
>   what he saw and experienced. The pilgrimage of a
>   disciple began!"

It is just as the scriptures declare, "If any one is in Christ, there is a new creation. The old has passed away; behold everything is new." I have experienced that, and I have seen it repeated thousands of times. It is life's greatest miracle – the miracle of a life made new by Christ.

The second miracle is one which Motel celebrates in his song. It is the miracle of growth. Motel surprised himself when he was able to muster the courage to ask for Tzeitel's hand in marriage. Love is a powerful motivator and Tzeitel had encouraged him. Then, when Tevye said, "Yes," Motel was so overjoyed that he began to dance and sing,

> "Wonder of wonders, miracle of miracles, I was afraid
> that God would frown,
> But like he did so long ago in Jericho God has made a
> wall fall down.
> When Moses softened Pharaoh's heart, that was a
> miracle.
> When God made the waters of the Red Sea part, that
> was a miracle too;

But of all God's miracles large and small, the most
miraculous one of all,
Is that out of a worthless lump of clay, God has made a
man today!"

That is something worth celebrating, isn't it? We all come into this world as little bundles of potential. At the outset, the potential is undeveloped, so we spend a life-time experiencing, learning, and growing. I can't think of anything more exciting than that. One reason we are so captivated by babies is that, when we look into their faces, we know that we are looking at all kinds of possibilities. That is the way we all start, and no matter how long we live, we never graduate from the school of life. We never arrive at our destination. No matter how much growing we do, there is always more growing to be done!

The fact that we can grow and become is part of God's good news for every person.

The good news is that what we are right now is not the final word. There is still the chance to become! Some time ago I was digging through some old papers and discovered a photograph of me just after Patricia and I were married. I looked at that six foot tall, one hundred thirty pound weakling and I began to give thanks for the possibility of growth. Periodically I read through a sermon I wrote early in my ministry and I thank God for growth! I remember some of the dumb things I have said and some of the thoughtless things I have done and I am overjoyed to know that life doesn't always have to be like that. I can learn. I can develop skills. I can deepen relationships. I can grow!

That is what Motel was celebrating. He was a poor tailor, a shy mousy guy almost afraid of his own shadow, but he loved Tzeitel. Motivated by his love, he reached deep inside himself and discovered a courage he never knew he had. He approached Tevye, asked for Tzeitel's hand in marriage and, wonder of wonders, Tevye said, "Yes." The mouse had become a man! It's the miracle of growth!

As important as it was for Motel to sing about the miracle of growth, it was even more important for him to sing about the miracle of relationship. He could hardly believe it, but his dream was coming true. His entire life was taking on new meaning because he was going to marry the love of his life. Listen to what he sang,

"Wonder of wonders, miracle of miracles, God took a
   tailor by the hand,
Turned him around and miracle of miracles, led him
   to the promised land.
When David slew Goliath, Yes! That was a miracle.
   When God gave us manna in the wilderness, that
   was a miracle too.
But of all God's miracles, large and small, the most
   miraculous one of all
Is one I thought could never be: God has given you to
   me."

In those words, Motel sang about one of the deepest meanings of
life. In all of my searching, I have not been able to find a better word to
describe the essence of life than the word, "relationship." I believe that
we were created to live in a loving, trusting relationship with God, and
in caring, mutually helping relationships with others. I am convinced
that life is either good or less than good for us depending upon the
quality of those relationships.

Do you remember Arthur Miller dealing with it in his classic play,
"Death of a Salesman?" Two friends were talking. Biff says, "Are you
content, Hap? You're a success, aren't you? Are you content?" Hap says
sadly, "No." "Why? You're making money aren't you?" Hap replies, "All I
can do now is wait for the merchandising manager to die. And suppose
I get to be merchandising manager? He's a good friend of mine, and
he just built a terrific estate on Long Island. And he lived there two
months and sold it, and now he's building another one. He can't enjoy
it once it's finished. And I know that's just what I would do. I don't know
what...I'm working for. Sometimes I sit in my apartment – all alone.
And I think of the rent I'm paying. And it's crazy. But then, it's what I
always wanted: my own apartment, a car...and still...I'm lonely."

The story is always the same, isn't it? You can have everything else
worth having, but if you don't have loving relationships, you really don't
have the most important thing – the thing that makes everything else
more valuable.

The most depressing sight in the world is someone who is all alone,
with no one to care whether he lives or dies. All of the joyful experiences
in life lose their joy when we don't have anyone with whom to share

them. All of the difficult and painful experiences of life are doubly devastating if we must endure them alone. It is absolutely true that the essence of life has to do with relationship. Every person needs to have someone who cares and gives them that most priceless of gifts, the gift of love.

Even fussbudget Lucy, in the "Peanuts" cartoon strip knows that she needs love. In one of the strips, Lucy is sitting by Schroeder's piano, listening to him play. Suddenly, she interrupts his music with a question, "Schroeder, do you love me a bushel and a peck?" Without batting an eye, he answers firmly, "No!" Lucy pauses just for a moment to think, and then asks, "How about a meter and a liter?" Even Lucy refuses to give up in her search for love because she senses how much she needs it.

I am sure that, on any list of God's great gifts, very near the top must be this gift of relationship. Without it, our lives are impoverished, but in the company of those we love, all life opens up and we begin to see, hear, and feel things we never knew were there before. Do you suppose that is God's strategy for His world? There are so many sights He wants us to see, but we will never see them alone. There are so many gifts God wants to give us, but we will never receive them if we are alone. There are so many good experiences God wants us to have, but they are available to us only in the company of someone we love.

That is why we sing about relationships in terms of wonders and miracles. Loving relationships become the doorway through which we can enter the fullness of life.

There is a song from "The Music Man" by Meredith Wilson which says it beautifully. Not only is it a memorable love song, it is so full of meaning that it is the title song of a previous chapter. As you read the words again, think about the wonders and miracles God has given you in your life, and use these words as an occasion of gratitude.

> "There were bells on the hill, but I never heard them ringing,
> No, I never heard them at all, 'til there was you.
> There were birds in the sky, but I never saw them winging,
> No, I never saw them at all, 'til there was you.
> And there was music, and there were wonderful roses,

They tell me, in sweet fragrant meadows of dawn and
dew.
There was love all around, but I never heard it singing,
No, I never heard it at all, 'til there was you."

Wonder of wonders, miracle of miracles! There is God. There is
growth. There is relationship. As a result, life is very good!

Prayer: Father, we are grateful for Your many gifts which we receive
as expressions of Your love. Help us to open our eyes to the wonders
and miracles of life all around us. Enable us to see Your gracious and
life giving hand at work in them all. As a result, help us to celebrate the
sheer joy of living. In Jesus' name we pray. Amen.

Tomorrow

I Peter 1:3-7

Little Orphan Annie was a cartoon strip character long before she was a Broadway star. I grew up with Annie, her dog Sandy, Daddy Warbucks, Punjab, and the whole cast. But I didn't know Annie's whole story until I saw and heard the Broadway musical.

The production is set in the midst of the Great Depression. Annie's parents had left her at an orphanage because they were unable to care for her. All she had from her parents was half a locket and a note saying that they would return for her when they could. She believed with all her heart that someday they would return and keep their promise. She lived by that hope. Her specific hopes were never realized because her parents had died before they could come for her. But Annie's hope for tomorrow motivated her every single day and shaped her life in positive ways. She always saw the glass half full. She expected that good things would come her way...tomorrow. Ultimately she experienced a happy ending when she was adopted by Daddy Warbucks, a billionaire industrialist. Annie and Daddy Warbucks each needed someone to love and someone to be loved by, and in the end, they found that wonderfully in each other.

All through the musical, Annie refused to be a victim of her circumstances. From deep within her, she brought something vibrant and positive to whatever circumstances she encountered. She brought

hope wherever she went by her vision of "tomorrow." Clearly, she was
the single most positive influence in the lives of the other children at
the orphanage. Early in the musical the orphans sang about their "hard
knock life." They sang:

> "It's the hard knock life for us! 'Steada treated, we get
>   tricked,
> 'Steada kisses, we get kicked. It's the hard knock life!
> Got no folks to speak of, so, it's the hard knock row we
>   hoe;
> Cotton blankets, 'steada wool, empty bellies 'steada
>   full. It's the hard knock life!
> Don't it feel like the wind is always howlin? Don't it
>   seem like there's never any light?
> Once a day don't you wanna throw the towel in? It's
>   easier than puttin' up a fight.
> No one's there when your dreams get creepy,
> No one cares if you grow or if you shrink; no one dries
>   when your eyes get wet and weepy,
> From the cryin' you would think this place'd sink!
>   Santa Claus we never see,
> Santa Claus? Who's that? Who's he? No one cares for
>   you a smidge when you're in an orphanage. It's the
>   hard knock life!"

Annie knew all of that to be true. But she refused to be defeated
by it. Each day she was sustained by hope - and she sang about it. Let's
listen...

> "The sun'll come out tomorrow,
> Bet your bottom dollar that tomorrow there'll be sun,
> Just thinkin' about tomorrow
> Clears away the cobwebs and the sorrow 'til there's
> none.
> When I'm stuck with a day that's gray and lonely
> I just stick out my chin and grin and say, Oh,
> The sun'll come out tomorrow,
> So you got to hang on 'til tomorrow, come what may!

Tomorrow, tomorrow, I love you, tomorrow,
You're always a day away."

Although she was living in difficult and even oppressive
circumstances, Annie refused to be a victim. She was able to overcome
her circumstances by what she brought to those circumstances. Her
life was shaped not by what she *found* out there, but by what she
brought with her to *whatever* was out there. As I think about Annie,
I remember something Victor Frankl wrote. Frankl was a survivor of
a Nazi concentration camp. He wrote about his experience in a book
which he named, "Man's Search for Meaning". He wrote about those
remarkable people in the camps who rose above their circumstances
by comforting others and giving away their last pieces of bread. Others
succumbed to their circumstances and became filled with despair, often
becoming ill or even dying because of their lack of hope. His experience
in the camp convinced him of what he called "the last human freedom."
He said that everything else can be taken from us, but no one can take
away our freedom to choose what attitude we will bring to any set of
circumstances!

That was Annie. She was not a victim of circumstances, but a victor
over circumstances because of her hope for tomorrow. Annie makes me
consider the various ways we approach tomorrow – the future. Let me
cite three ways of dealing with tomorrow.

First, a great many people use tomorrow as a way to avoid living
today. I am convinced that one of the most destructive human failings
is the tendency to procrastinate: "Never do today what you can put off
'til tomorrow."

Procrastination is one of the most effective ways to assuage our
conscience. When there is something we think we ought to do and we
don't want to do it, our conscience would bother us if we simply and
honestly said, "I don't want to do that. I refuse!" So, instead of that, we
say to ourselves, "I ought to do it, and I will do it, one of these days."
And, of course, it never gets done.

We say, "I'm going to heal that broken relationship, one of these
days; I'm going to break that life destroying habit, one of these days; I'm
going to give more time and attention to my family, one of these days;
I'm going to write that letter, make that telephone call, or sit down face
to face with someone and tell them how much I love and appreciate

them, one of these days; I'm going to stop playing games with God and make a serious commitment of my life to Him, one of these days."

We have so many noble, thoughtful, and loving impulses. We possess so many good intentions, but the road to "you know where" is paved with those. Isn't it sad that so many of our best ideas are never acted upon? We think them, we feel them, and then we set them aside for tomorrow.

Recently I read a story that touched me. It was written by a country preacher who told of a death in his congregation. A wife and mother had died suddenly while she was at work at the kitchen sink. She was a good and loving woman who had raised a large family. And then, suddenly, she was gone. At the funeral, her husband did not cry or seem to grieve in any discernable way. He was a hard working man and he seldom allowed his emotions to show. On the day of the funeral, he lingered to talk to his minister after the service. He pulled a small, shabby book out of his pocket and handed it to the pastor. He said, "It's a book of poems. She liked them very much. Would you read one for her now? She always wanted us to read them together, but I never seemed to have time. You know how it is on the farm. There are always so many things to be done." Then he added some words which have stuck in my mind. He said, "I guess you don't get it into your head what time is really for until it's too late."

The tragedy of procrastination is that the opportunity or the inclination may not come again, or, if they come again, it may be too late. I remember a poem that says it:

> "He was going to be all that a mortal should be…
>   tomorrow.
> No one would be kinder or braver than he…tomorrow.
> A friend who was troubled and weary, he knew, who'd
>   be glad of a lift, and needed it too,
> On him he would call and see what he could do…
>   tomorrow.
> Each morning he stacked up the letters he'd write…
>   tomorrow,
> And thought of the folks he would fill with delight…
>   tomorrow,
> It was too bad indeed, he was busy today, and hadn't a
>   minute to stop on his way,

More time he would have to give others, he'd say…
  tomorrow.
The greatest of workers this man would have been…
  tomorrow.
The world would have known him, had he ever seen…
  tomorrow.
But the fact is he died and faded from view, and all
  that he left herewhen living was through,
Was a mountain of things he intended to do…
  tomorrow!"

How sad! That's the danger of procrastination. Too many of us use tomorrow as an escape from the responsibilities and opportunities of today.

Second, a great many people look at tomorrow and see only problems there. For them, the future is an unknown that fills them with fear. They are unable to see the glass half full; it's always half empty. Such people can't enjoy even good circumstances because of what they fear *might* happen. With every silver lining they manage to find a dark cloud!

These are the "Yes, but…" people. No matter what good, hopeful, and optimistic thing you might say, their response is always, "Yes, but…" "It's a beautiful day isn't it?" "Yes, but it might still rain." "You have a wonderful family!" "Yes, but it is certainly expensive to provide for them." It is always "Yes, but…"

I don't know of anything more inhibiting and life-denying than fear. When we are afraid, we try to "play it safe," limit our liabilities, and, consequently, live our lives at a very shallow level. We are afraid to trust; we might be betrayed. We are afraid to love; we might be hurt. We allow our fear to dominate and we miss out on life at its best. One of the most important gifts Jesus has given to the world is liberation from fear so that we can live what he called "the abundant life." When we follow Jesus, we are able to put our hearts out there at risk because, in faith, we are able to look at tomorrow without fear.

One thing I say repeatedly both in preaching and in teaching is that, in the gospel, the opposite of faith is not unbelief; the opposite of faith is fear. Because of faith, we are able to trust in God to provide for all our tomorrows, so we don't have to live in fear. That is why, again and again in scripture, we are encouraged, "Don't be anxious." "Fear not." "Let not your heart be troubled." Because of God, and because He is the *kind of God* we have come to know and trust in Jesus, we don't have to be afraid.

One thing I have learned during my life is that our attitudes shape our lives. There is a "self fulfilling prophecy" at work. When, because of fear, we see the future as a problem, that way of seeing helps to *make* the future a problem. What you look for, you tend to find. What you expect, you help make happen. You become like the pessimist who wrote the epitaph for his headstone, "I expected this, and here I am." You can't live the best if you expect the worst.

As I have said, some look at tomorrow as an escape from today. Some look at tomorrow and expect only problems. Those are two ways of looking at the future, but I thank God that those are not the only options. For those able to see with the eyes of faith, the future is not a problem, but a promise. Because that future belongs to God we trust that God will make the future good.

People of faith believe that this is God's world. He made it, He sustains it, He is at work in it, and He will insure that the ultimate outcome is good because He is in charge here. It is true that not everything that happens is according to God's intention. God has given us freedom and He never withdraws that gift. So, we sometimes use our freedom, either intentionally or accidentally, to thwart God's good will for us. But ultimately God's love and goodness will win.

Do you believe that? How we look at the future makes so much difference because our vision of the future profoundly affects the way we live today. If we believe that history is wandering aimlessly, if we believe that the future is a dark and friendless unknown, if we believe that we step into tomorrow all alone – if we believe that we will be fearful, and for good reason! When fear is dominant, every day is lived under a cloud of apprehension.

But that is not the way we Christians see the future. We see the future as hopeful possibility. Our key word is "hope." Whatever our circumstances right now, they do not have the final word. The final word is never spoken until it is God's word. Whatever your reality is right now, it is only prelude to a new and better future if we will believe and allow God to provide. We Christians are able to believe that because we believe that a good, loving, and powerful God is for us and not against us. We believe that God holds the future in His hands and that He will go with us into that future to shape it into something good.

The reason Christians believe that is because of the resurrection of Christ. That is what Peter was writing about. Peter knew that the Christians had some rough days ahead. Many were going to be persecuted for their faith, and some were going to be put to death. Those first century Christians understood that their faith did not spare them from trouble; in some ways it even increased their troubles. Those who say that faith always ushers in an idyllic, problem free life are lying to us. That is not the promise. We are not always protected from troubles, but we are given all that we need to cope with and even to overcome our troubles. That is why, in the face of persecution and death, Peter talked about Jesus' resurrection. It is true that Jesus was put to death. He had said, honestly, "In the world you have tribulation..." As one translation puts it, "In the world you are going to take a beating." That's true. You can't live very long in this world without being hurt. Saying that is just observing life honestly. Jesus was put to death, but death was not able to hold him. God raised Jesus from the dead, and that resurrection shouted in unmistakable language that this is God's world and He is in charge here! Jesus' resurrection was vindication of all that was incarnate in him. Love, truth, justice and righteousness were resurrected too. On the day of crucifixion Jesus and all that he stood for seemed weak and defeated. But the view of history that comes to us on a given day is often deceiving. What we learned on the day of resurrection is that Jesus and all that he stood for can be nailed to a cross, wrapped in grave clothes, and sealed in a tomb, but we can be sure that they will rise again because they are of God! Hear the truth of faith: *God will not be defeated*, and all those who place themselves in the powerful hands of God are secure, not only for tomorrow, but for forever!

Peter summed it up by saying, "We have been born anew to a living hope through the resurrection of Jesus Christ from the dead." For those first century Christians, tomorrow was not a problem; it was a promise, because it was God's tomorrow. And, by living with that vision of tomorrow, they literally marched through the problems and perils of their day!

It makes so much difference how you see tomorrow, because it shapes how you will live today. *The* basic question of life is: do you live by fear or do you live by faith?

Although the musical, "Annie" doesn't talk about God or the resurrection, Annie's outlook seems much like that produced by faith: "The sun'll come out tomorrow!" When we live by faith, even a cloudy, problem filled day is filled with hope for a better tomorrow, and that hope gives us new life!

One final image. There was a note written by a woman in a concentration camp. She had found some seeds and planted them. She wrote, "All the seeds have failed except one. I don't know what it is, but I wait for a flower and not a weed."

Do you hear the hope in that? How can we live without it? Of course, the answer is that people of faith don't have to. Listen: "We have been born anew to a living hope through the resurrection of Jesus Christ from the dead."

Prayer: Loving Father, we are grateful for that vision of tomorrow which enables us to live fully today. Deliver us from fear and give us hope, because we see Your loving and powerful hand at work in all out tomorrows. In Jesus' name we pray. Amen.

The Impossible Dream

Matthew 5:38-48

The musical, "Man of La Mancha", opened on Broadway in November of 1965. When it was first announced, there was very little excitement about it. After all, people thought, it is just another staging of the old Don Quixote story. But when the final curtain came down there were cheers, and a standing ovation which has few parallels in modern theatrical history. The critics predicted that it was a musical which would endure for generations!

I am sure you know the story. Don Quixote was a man with a touch of madness who set out on a quest. He had an impossible dream which was "to right the unrightable wrong, to reach the unreachable star." He was driven by a vision of what ought to be, and he felt called to work against overwhelming odds to make things what they ought to be.

For example, when he looked at Aldonza, the part-time prostitute, part-time servant girl at the inn, he saw in her a beauty that no one else saw. In his mind, she was his lady and he called her by another name, "Dulcinea." "Lady indeed," everyone thought, "it's only Aldonza. Everyone knows Aldonza!" But Quixote knelt before her and asked for a token of her affection to take with him into battle. In derision, she gave him a cleaning rag, dirty and full of holes. Everyone laughed, including Aldonza. But Quixote thanked her and tenderly kissed the foul smelling rag before affixing it to his lance. Everyone ridiculed this mad old man with his crazy dreams, but something was stirred in Aldonza. No one had ever seen her as Quixote did. No one had ever spoken to her as he did. Something deep was stirred in her, while the jeers of the surrounding crowd continued. In the midst of the jeers, Don Quixote sang of his dream...

> "To dream the impossible dream, to fight the
>   unbeatable foe,
> To bear with unbearable sorrow, to run where the
>   brave dare not go;
> To right the unrightable wrong, to love pure and
>   chaste from afar
> To try when your arms are too weary to reach the
>   unreachable star,
> This is my quest, to follow that star, no matter how
>   hopeless, no matter how far,
> To fight for the right without question or pause, to be
>   willing to march into hell for a heavenly cause;
> And I know if I'll only be true to this glorious quest,
>   that my heart will lie peaceful and calm when I'm
>   laid to my rest.
> And the world will be better for this, that one man
>   scorned and covered with scars,
> Still strove with his last ounce of courage, to reach the
>   unreachable stars."

In the Broadway opening, when Quixote had finished his song, the audience stood and cheered with tears in their eyes. What, do you suppose, got to them? What moved them so deeply? I believe they were touched by the appeal of a great dream, an ideal, even if it is called "impossible." At least for awhile, that sophisticated Broadway audience was caught up in Quixote's quest. They immersed themselves in risky, romantic idealism and they loved it! That is noteworthy because idealism is now out of style. We pride ourselves in being realists. We evaluate everything in terms of efficiency, cost effectiveness and practicality. Many of us have little time for dreams or visions. We are practical people and we are proud of it!

That is why we have trouble with the Sermon on the Mount from the fifth chapter of the gospel of Matthew. O, we can get sentimental about it. We can profess to believe it. But when it comes down to putting it into practice, we are more practical and realistic than that.

Common sense tells us that to go two miles when you are required to go only one is ridiculous. To turn the other cheek when someone is hitting us is foolish. To pray for those who are persecuting us is dumb. To love our enemies makes no sense. And, at the end of all these impractical commandments for Jesus to tell us to be perfect is the supreme irrationality! Who among us can be perfect? Who can do any of these things that Jesus is asking us to do? We don't deny that they are beautiful thoughts and in an ideal world, even desirable ones. But in our kind of world, among people like us, no way! We are more practical than that. It's true, isn't it? With most of us, idealism is out of style.

I believe, however, that is precisely what is killing us. Too much has gone wrong with our world because we have become so calculating and "practical" that we have set aside our dreams and ideals. We seldom ask for and expect the best from others. And worse, we seldom expect the best from ourselves.

Jesus reminds us that you cannot live the best if you expect the worst. What we need is a dream, a vision of what can be. We need a dream that captures our imagination and inspires us to reach again and again for that which can yet be by God's grace. When Jesus talked about giving us "abundant life," he wasn't talking about routine "practicality" or business as usual. He was talking about a dream of what can be!

Listen now, I'm about to say something important: when we are open to it, God gives us a dream of the person we can become by His grace, and a dream of all the loving, helpful, and life-giving things we can do as followers of Jesus. Then God begins to work in us and through us to make that dream come true. When Jesus says, "Be perfect," he is not talking about conformity to an abstract set of standards. He is not talking about "cookie cutter" Christians where we all come out looking and acting the same. No, when Jesus talked about perfection, he was talking about completion. To be perfect means to be complete, the complete "you," to be the person that God intended when He created you.

So, here is the plan: when God created you, He had in mind the person you would become, and, He built into you all that you need to become that person. Once we say, "Yes" to God, He begins to work in us, shaping us and molding us into the person He created us to be. It is a lifelong process of becoming, and we never complete the process. No matter how much we grow, as long as we live we will have more growing to do. So, that is what perfection is: it's completion; it's becoming a finished product. But, because God never completes our becoming, perfection is something we work toward, not something we ever fully achieve!

There are two things we would do well to avoid in this process. First, avoid the notion that we *have* to be perfect. I can think of few things worse than feeling that we are nobodies, unworthy of love from God or anyone else until we become perfect. It's miserable to believe that we cannot make mistakes, that we cannot forgive ourselves for imperfections or that we cannot have a moment's rest until we become perfect. To live that kind of neurotic, compulsive, and driven life is to be in hell!

I once knew a young girl who became emotionally ill and was hospitalized because she was convinced that no one would accept her unless she became perfect. She placed an impossible demand upon herself. This *compulsion* to be perfect is not what Jesus was talking about. We are not called to join the rat race striving for perfection. The Christian gospel does not say, "Become perfect so that God will love us." No, the gospel affirms the opposite. God loves us just as we are. It's an unconditional gift. Because of that gift, we can be free from anxiety and compulsion, so that God can work with His grace to take us from where we are and move us in the direction of perfection, completion.

So the first thing to avoid is the notion that you *have* to be perfect, either to satisfy God's demands or to earn His love. I like the bumper sticker that says, "Christians are not perfect, we're just forgiven." We are not perfect. God loves and accepts us just as we are. But, because God loves us He does not leave us as we are. When the right thing is happening, God is at work in us moving us toward completion.

The second thing to avoid is using God's love as an excuse for inertia, as a reason for not growing. Just because God loves us as we are doesn't mean that we should be satisfied with where we are. We must settle for nothing less than perpetual growth. We must settle for nothing less than becoming all that God has created us to be. It is true that, at any given moment, God loves us just as we are. But, instead of using His love as a pillow to sleep on, we are called to use it as a stepping stone to newness and as a means of becoming all we can be.

I keep saying it: perfection is not a demand that God places upon us so much as it is a promise that God makes to us. Please understand once and for all that God is not a God *out there* placing rules and responsibilities upon us or making us jump through religious hoops to earn and deserve His acceptance. No, God is a God *in here*, loving us, and helping us to grow and become all that He has created us to be. Don't settle for anything less!

When we think about the dream God wants to give us, we must understand that it may not be particularly important whether or not that dream is fully attainable in this life. I admire those artisans who worked all their lives on the great cathedrals of Europe, knowing all the while that the work would not be completed in their lifetimes. The worth of an ideal is better measured by the direction it gives to life.

It happened many years ago, but I still remember when Bob Beamon broke the long jump record in the 1968 Olympics. He broke the previous record not by inches, but by almost two feet! When someone asked him about it, he acknowledged that, although he jumped more than twenty-nine feet, he was trying to jump thirty-one feet! In a sense, he failed. He did not reach his goal, but he set a new world record and jumped farther than anyone in history because he reached for the unreachable!

There was a woman who learned that she had a disabling illness and had to be confined to her bed for a long period of time. She decided to devote her long hours to writing a novel. It was never published and few people read it. In a sense, she failed to reach her goal, but her writing saved her sanity and gave her a sense of purpose during her confinement.

You get the idea: the worth of an ideal must not be measured only by the extent to which we attain it. Just the reaching for it can give life a noble direction. One thing that excites me about the Christian gospel is that it challenges us to reach for the unreachable. We will never outgrow our ideals, because no matter how much we grow and accomplish, Christ will still be out there ahead of us, calling us to grow some more and to accomplish more. That excites me. I don't want to follow a Jesus who asks me to be less than my best. I would not be impressed with a Jesus who allowed me to be satisfied with myself as I am. The thing that impresses and excites me is that Jesus says, "Be perfect!" That is a dream worthy of us.

It's important to me to be able to go home at night, look in the mirror, and be comfortable with what I see and not embarrassed to look myself in the eye. It's important for me to know that I have reached for the best and that I have tried to be my best. Then I can go to sleep in peace. As Quixote sang, "I know if I'll only be true to this glorious quest, that my heart will lie peaceful and calm when I'm laid to my rest."

The good news is that when we reach for the unreachable, everything is changed as a result of our reaching. We cannot fully live up to the high standards of the Sermon on the Mount. Perfection and completion will not be achieved in our lifetime but that is no reason not to try. The person who reaches for the highest ideals, even if he fails, still changes his life for the better by the trying.

Think about Simon Peter, a rough, crude, and impetuous fisherman. Before meeting Jesus he was a man of little consequence and no one expected him to be anything more, especially him. Then Jesus came along, tapped him on the shoulder and said, "Follow me and I will teach you how to fish for people." Later, when Simon had grown in his vision and understanding, he professed his faith in Jesus as "the Christ." Jesus said, "You are Peter, the rock, and on this rock I will build my church." Up to that point, Simon had not acted much like a rock, but Jesus gave him a new vision of himself. Simon began to believe in that vision and it changed his life. Although he never became perfect, the more he saw himself as Peter, the rock, the more he became Peter, the rock.

As he did throughout his ministry, Jesus believed Simon Peter into newness. Jesus saw something that was not yet reality, and made that vision come true. That sort of thing has happened so many times in history that I have begun to wonder - just how realistic is our so-called realism? It may be that calculating, hard-headed and practical realism simply encourages mediocrity. What we need is more dreams, more visions of the way things ought to be, especially when it is God who gives us the dreams and promises to be with us on our quest. When we see things in that way, we begin to believe that Jesus knew what he was talking about when he said, "Be perfect."

In "Man of La Mancha", the people were making fun of that crazy old man, Quixote, with his impossible dreams. Aldonza joined in the jeers, but Quixote's words stirred a longing within her. Gradually the dream of the person she could become began to grow in her.

Near the end of the story, Quixote had abandoned his quest. His energy was depleted, his hope was gone, and he was lying at home, disillusioned and dying. When Aldonza heard about it, she went to his side and pleaded with him to become Don Quixote again and to restore in her the lost vision. "Remember," she said, "you once called me by another name. Bring back the dream of Dulcinea, the bright and shining Dulcinea." She helped him recall the words of his song. He was stirred and got up from his bed. He imagined setting out again on his quest. With excitement and new energy he began to sing, "I am the man of La Mancha!" But the strain was too much. He collapsed and died.

Aldonza refused to accept his death. She said, "A man has died. He seemed a good man, but I did not know him. Don Quixote is not dead." Just then someone addressed her as "Aldonza." With a lift of her chin, she replied, "My name is Dulcinea," and Dulcinea she became.

Those standing near were so moved by what they saw that they began to sing Quixote's song,

> "This is my quest, to follow that star, no matter how
>   hopeless, no matter how far,
> To fight for the right without question or pause, to be
>   willing to march into hell for a heavenly cause;
> And I know if I'll only be true to this glorious quest,
>   that my heart will lie peaceful and calm when I'm
>   laid to my rest.
> And the world will be better for this, that one man
>   scorned and covered with scars,
> Still strove with his last ounce of courage, to reach the
>   unreachable stars."

Do you hear it? It's just as Jesus said two thousand years ago, "Be perfect, just as your heavenly Father is perfect."

Prayer: Give us a dream, O God, Your dream. Give us the courage to reach for those Godly ideals which are unreachable, so that all of life can be changed for the better, and so that we may be Your faithful people. We pray in the name of the one who gives us the heavenly vision and who accompanies us as we reach for it – Jesus, the Christ. Amen.

You'll Never Walk Alone

Ephesians 2:19-20

"Carousel" has never been one of my favorite Broadway musicals, but it does contain one of my all-time favorite songs and I want to conclude this book with it. The song is, "You'll Never Walk Alone."

In the musical, Billy Bigelow was a handsome, carefree, self-centered barker at a local carousel. A barker was the man out front, talking up the ride and recruiting customers. Billy's good looks and engaging personality enabled him to entice the young girls to spend their money and ride the carousel. Billy fell in love with and married his high school sweetheart, Julie Jordan, but he was too immature and irresponsible both for marriage and parenthood. Things did not go well. When he and Julie had a daughter, the owner of the carousel thought that he could no longer be effective as the barker at the carousel as a married man with a daughter. As a result, Billy was fired.

Soon the money ran out and Billy could not provide for his family. He attempted a robbery in which he was shot and killed. There had not been much about Billy's life that was admirable. I have already used the words, "self-centered" and "irresponsible." That pretty well sums it up. The most redeeming quality of his life was that he did love his daughter. From the other side of death, Billy saw that she was lonely, unhappy, and in danger of making some choices that would ruin her life. Though he could not communicate with her in the same ways we communicate, he found a way to reach out to her and help her. It is a deeply moving moment in the musical when this father, with great love for his daughter, begins to sing to her. Listen…

> "When you walk through a storm, hold your head up high,
> And don't be afraid of the dark;
> At the end of the storm is a golden sky, and the sweet, silver sound of a lark.
> Walk on through the wind, walk on through the rain,
> Though your dreams be tossed and blown;
> Walk on, walk on, with hope in your heart, and you'll never walk alone,
> You'll never walk alone."

Billy was saying to his daughter that love would not let them finally be separated, and that he would always be with her. Was that only a dream, or was it reality? His daughter didn't know for sure, and neither do we. But there are some things I believe.

I believe in them so strongly that I am willing to bet my life upon them.

There is no feeling quite as devastating as the feeling that we are all alone. Few things in life are more important than having people who know us, care about us, and are willing to help us. It gives us a good, warm, and secure feeling to know that we are in caring relationships. That is what families are supposed to be – people who know us and love us and will never forsake us, no matter what. That is what caring friendships are supposed to be – people we trust enough to unpack our hearts to them, and know that they are for us and with us unconditionally. That is what the church is at its best.

That is one reason the text from Ephesians is good news. Paul is saying to the Christians at Ephesus, "You are no longer strangers, but fellow citizens with the saints, and members of the household of God." In other words, you are not alone. You are family. You belong! I believe that we can face anything and we can deal with anything as long as we are not alone. As long as we face it with those we love and who love us we can prevail.

That should come as good news to each of us, because there are times when we feel very much alone. That is particularly true when someone we love has died; it is what Billy Bigelow's daughter felt. When a loved one dies, we feel that loss keenly because it seems that a part of us has been taken away, and it feels like nothing can ever fill that empty place their death has left.

Nothing should be said in these pages to deny the reality of our grief or the appropriateness of our grief. Our love gives us the right to grieve. And the fact is, the more we love someone, the more we feel it. It is important to remember, however, that the pain we feel at a loved one's death is the other side of the joy we experienced during their life. If we had not loved so much, we would not hurt so much. Were it not for the joy we experienced during their life, we would not be feeling such grief at their death. So, I never want to reduce the sorrow of death by any degree, because the only way to do that would be to reduce the love and joy we experienced during their life. That is too high a price to pay. I invite you to wear your grief like a badge of honor, attesting to the love and joy we have shared! Grief and loneliness are real, they are normal, and they are appropriate.

But those are not the only realities. There are other realities we can grasp when a loved one dies to give us strength and hope and even a kind of quiet joy. The power of their influence is one such reality. Think about the beautiful reality that our lives are shaped for good by those who love us, and that is something that can never be taken away from us, not even by death. So, who we are, what we believe and value, and how we act will always bear the imprint of our loving relationships, even if those relationships have been interrupted by death. Our loved ones will always be with us through their influence.

Memory is another positive reality. I believe that memory is one of God's greatest gifts to us. It's instinctive. When someone dies, instinctively we begin to remember and to share our memories. Someone will say, "I remember when..." and everyone will laugh. Someone else will say, "Do you remember the time..." and some will cry. As we instinctively remember and share memories something strengthening and healing is taking place. Aren't you glad that the good times of life are not ours just for the moment and then over and done with? Instead, the good times can be re-lived again and again through memory. I like the way Sir James Barrie, the author of Peter Pan, said it, "God gave us memory so that we may have roses in December." The more we remember, the more the past becomes present, and our loved one is with us again, through memory.

In writing to first century Christians, Paul reminded them that they belonged to a fellowship built on the foundation of the apostles and prophets, with Jesus Christ himself as the chief cornerstone. They remembered. They sensed the strength of their fellowship. And, as they remembered, Christ was there and they received grace and strength from him.

The Christian gospel has always insisted that love can defy boundaries of space and time. Nothing can separate us from the love of God, and nothing can finally separate us from those we love - not even death.

I hope you have experienced the reality of that, as I have. For nineteen years, Patricia, Mark, Lynne and I lived in Arizona and California, while the rest of our family lived many miles away in Mississippi. We saw them once a year and talked with them regularly by telephone. I will always remember how my parents assured me of their love, especially my mother. When we talked on the telephone, almost invariably she would say before hanging up, "Just know that I am always with you. Nothing can separate me from my boy!"

In one sense, that was a foolish statement. I was in California, she was in Mississippi, and we were separated by many miles. But that is a shallow understanding of reality. As I listened to her, I knew she was right. My parents are a part of me and they always will be. I remembered all the good times we had shared, I recalled the assurances of their love, and as I remembered all of that, time and space disappeared, and we were together. It is true. Love defies boundaries of space and time. We were together through memory and love.

I hasten to add that the experiences I am talking about are not limited to memory. My parents died years ago, so now we are separated not just by miles, but by death, just as you are separated from loved ones by death. Still, I believe in the power of love to defy boundaries of time and space. I believe that my parents are with me still!

I believe in life after death. I believe that the loving relationships which begin in this life are continued in the life to come. I trust in the promise of Jesus who said, "Because I live, you too shall live."

Either that is true, or as far as I am concerned, nothing in life makes any sense. For me, the sanity of life is called into question if we simply live out our few short years and then disappear into nothingness. That doesn't make any sense! Why would God create us, encourage us to develop our minds, abilities, and interests, and invite us into loving relationships, only to have the whole thing disappear into nothingness through death? No, I will not believe that's the way it is. There is something deep within each of us that rebels against that and cries out against that. I agree with Harry Emerson Fosdick who said, "God is not some crazy artist, who goes around painting pictures in order to erase them." Of course He isn't! Life does not end in death. The best in life is not at the mercy of the worst. The final word about us is not death, but life...eternal life. We prepare ourselves in this life for that which will continue in the next. For us, death is not cessation, but transition.

Transition to what, I am not altogether sure. And, I must admit that I am properly skeptical of those who tell us more than they know and begin to describe life after death in detail, such as the décor of heaven and the temperature of hell. Who among us can contain thoughts of any heaven worthy of the name within our little box of brains? I am simply willing to trust the promise of scripture, "Eye has not seen, nor ear heard, neither has it entered the heart of any human being, the things which God has prepared for those who love Him."

I can't tell you exactly what heaven will be like, but I believe that God will be there and that He will make it good. I believe that we will know each other. I believe that we will be restored to fullness of life and health, and that pain and sorrow and sickness and death will be no more. I believe that there will be a time of continuing growth and that we will have a long, long, long eternity to enjoy the loving relationships there.

Further, I believe that, once we die and are in heaven, there will be the possibility of a kind of relationship with the living. Scripture affirms that, and there are countless stories of people who have experienced it. When writing to the church at Ephesus, Paul told them that they were fellow citizens with the saints and members of the household of God. It was quite clear to them that the saints he was talking about were both those who were living and those who had died. The fellowship of Christians is, therefore, not limited to a particular time and space. Ours is a fellowship of eternal life. The members of the Christian family remain a part of it, even after death.

For centuries, Christians have referred to the one church which has two parts: the church militant and the church triumphant; that is, the church made up of those still living in this world, and the church made up of those who have died and are now in God's nearer presence. In the Apostle's Creed, we affirm our belief in "the communion of saints." In the communion liturgy we often say, "Therefore with angels and archangels and with all the company of heaven, we laud and magnify Your holy name."

Don't you see, whatever we do as Christians, we are never alone! Of course God is with us, and all the saints are with us too. (When I use the word, "saints," I am talking about all Christians, and especially those who have passed through death to new life in our Father's house.) As we gather for worship, all those Christians who lived in past generations are with us. As we struggle with difficulty, they are with us. And, as we seek to be faithful Christians, they are with us.

They are like our cheering section. As we are down on the playing field of life, those who have died and are in heaven are up in the stands cheering us on. We break through for a gain and they shout, "Yea!" We are thrown for a loss, and they say, "Get up and try again. We are with you. We are for you!" That's exciting to me, and it's strengthening too. It means so much to know that, at every moment we are in the presence of the apostles, Augustine, St. Francis, Luther, Wesley, our parents, and all the people of God of all ages. Wow! The Bible tells us that we are "surrounded by a great cloud of witnesses," and we live our lives on the foundations they have built and with the encouragement they provide. That gives me strength, encouragement, and hope. I am never alone, and neither are you!

Often, on All Saints Sunday, we read the names of members who have passed into the church triumphant. It is good to remember that their names are still written on our church membership rolls. They are still a part of the church family. Their names are listed in the same way all the others are listed, except it is noted that they are now with the Lord. They are in the church triumphant. A pastor once expressed my feelings very well when he said, "We've taken them off the mailing list not because we don't know their present address, but because the Post Office hasn't established mail delivery there yet."

The first congregation I served had a little cemetery just outside where they buried their dead. In my unseasoned youth, I complained about it. I thought that an "out of the way" cemetery would be better. That way, we would not have to be reminded constantly about the reality of death. But I was wrong. I now believe that we have lost something valuable by removing our burial sites from the church. The cathedrals of Europe have members buried beneath the floor. Many early Christians worshipped in the catacombs, surrounded by the bodies of their dead. There is wisdom in that, to be reminded of the foundation on which they were building, and of the eternal nature of the church.

If you go into church buildings in the Orthodox tradition, you will notice that most of them have domed sanctuaries. There in the center of the nave, where the congregation sits, suspended and hovering over the gathered congregation, is a likeness of Christ, risen, triumphant, and *present*! All around the dome, there are depictions of the Apostles and the saints. As these Christians gather for worship, there is no mistaking it: they are surrounded by a cloud of witnesses. They are in the presence of the whole church, past and present, and they know that they are never alone!

During my last pastorate in California, we began the practice of having communion every Sunday, the first Sunday of the month for everyone, the other Sundays in the chapel. Following the worship service, one of the ministers would go into the chapel and celebrate the sacrament with those who came from the sanctuary for that experience. Sometimes there were only a few people present, and some questioned the validity of a service with such a small attendance. There was an inside joke among the members of the ministerial staff. One would ask, "How many were at communion today?" Sometimes the answer would be, "Only two, or four, or six." Then the first minister would say, "But you forgot to count the angels and archangels and all the company of heaven. In reality there were millions and millions there!" We would say that and laugh. But down deep we knew that there was reality in what we said. We are not alone. And, the more we are aware of that, the more we are open to the experience of that and the more we feel inspired, strengthened, and motivated by that.

Let me say it as plainly as I know how. Not only do I believe in life after death; not only do I believe in the presence of God; I believe in the living presence of the entire church triumphant. I believe that we can sense their presence and be helped by them. So, we are not alone, not now, not ever!

That is what Billy Bigelow was trying to say to his daughter. He loved her so much that space and time had no dominion over them. That's why he sang, "Walk on, walk on, with hope in your heart, and you'll never walk alone. You'll never walk alone!"

Prayer: God, our Father, we thank you that through Jesus death has been defeated and we have been given assurance of life, eternal life. We are grateful for the timeless Christian family of which we are a part, and for the love that will bind us together both for now and for always. Help us now to be comforted, inspired, and strengthened by the assurance that we will never be alone – You and all those we love are with us, always. We pray with gratitude in the name of the risen and living Christ. Amen.

Made in the USA
Columbia, SC
20 April 2022